# WINDOWS XP
# TROUBLESHOOTING

STUART YARNOLD

## BARNES & NOBLE BOOKS
NEW YORK

**In easy steps** is an imprint of Computer Step
Southfield Road . Southam
Warwickshire CV47 0FB . United Kingdom
www.ineasysteps.com

This edition published for Barnes & Noble Books, New York
FOR SALE IN THE USA ONLY
www.bn.com

**Notice of Liability**
Every effort has been made to ensure that this book contains accurate
and current information. However, Computer Step and the author
shall not be liable for any loss or damage suffered by readers as a
result of any information contained herein.

**Trademarks**
Microsoft® and Windows® are registered trademarks of Microsoft
Corporation. All other trademarks are acknowledged as belonging to
their respective companies.

Printed and bound in the United Kingdom

ISBN 0-7607-6871-4

# Contents

## Internet/Email Troubleshooting

# 13

## Miscellaneous XP Problems Troubleshooting

# 14

## XP Service Pack 2 Troubleshooting

# 15

## Index

# Troubleshooting Techniques

Troubleshooting a computer can sometimes be like looking for a needle in a haystack, as there can be so many potential causes of a fault. Many faults are accompanied by incomprehensible and sometimes misleading error messages that further muddy the waters. Faced with this situation, all too many people blindly dive in with no real understanding of what they are doing, and succeed only in making matters worse.

This chapter points you in the right direction by explaining how to narrow down the problem, giving some basic troubleshooting procedures and things you should or should not do.

## Covers

**Chapter One**

# Introduction

*Never be afraid to attempt your own repairs and upgrades – it's a lot easier than you might think. All you need is a bit of common sense and this book!*

The purpose of Windows XP Troubleshooting is to provide concise, easy-to-follow troubleshooting guides covering all aspects of a computer system, including XP itself. Obviously, it's impossible to cover every conceivable fault, so the book is restricted to serious issues such as failure to start, plus the more common types of problem users are likely to experience.

Note that this is not a general "how to" book on XP. If this is what you are looking for then read no further – this title will not be for you. Try "Windows XP in easy steps" by the same publisher, which will give you a good grounding in XP and how to use it.

Clearly, the most serious issue that anyone is likely to encounter is a PC that refuses to start. There are any number of reasons why this can happen, a fact that makes it one of the most difficult computer faults to diagnose and repair. For this reason there are two chapters devoted entirely to this matter, and together they provide a comprehensive step-by-step guide to bringing your computer back from the dead.

*Something for you to think about – many of the problems that computer users experience are actually caused by them doing something incorrectly (or that they shouldn't be doing at all). All too often the operating system and associated hardware is blameless. Any computer technician will confirm this fact.*

Crashes and lockups, while less serious, are a common and irritating part of a PC user's life. See System Instability Troubleshooting for the low-down on this type of problem and what to do about it.

Millions of people use the Internet, and every single one of them, at one time or another, will have problems – logging on, broken connections, or sending and receiving email. The Modem and Internet/Email Troubleshooting chapters cover this subject in detail.

Each chapter examines a different part of the system, detailing common faults and a systematic procedure for isolating and repairing them. All relevant terminology is explained, so as to make the various procedures as clear as possible.

Please note that this book makes no attempt to troubleshoot specific problems with an item of hardware, but just shows you how to identify a particular hardware device as faulty. Having done so, it's up to you to get the device either repaired or replaced.

*Very rarely is it worth getting hardware repaired. It will probably cost as much as it would to replace the item, and you will be spending money to repair something that's almost certainly obsolete anyway. Computer technology advances rapidly.*

You will find that when troubleshooting a computer, you are dealing predominantly with software. As Windows is the main software application on a PC, this means that effectively you are either troubleshooting Windows itself or troubleshooting with Windows (for example, you may be using the Windows utility Chkdsk to check your hard disk for errors).

Hence the book's title, "Windows XP Troubleshooting:" even though it also covers hardware, it is about troubleshooting an XP computer system.

You will find no padding exercises, such as lengthy descriptions of how to clean a keyboard; the book assumes you are an intelligent human being and don't need to be told the blindingly obvious. Throughout this book you will find many page references: this is to avoid repetition, as so many faults can be caused by the same things.

The book contains a number of web addresses, all of which were correct at the time of going to press. However, we are unable to guarantee that these addresses will all still be valid by the time you read this.

*Absolutely the best aid to successful troubleshooting, whatever the subject, is knowledge. The more you know about computers – and there is a lot to know – the easier it will be to diagnose and repair faults. Take the time to acquire and read a few computer books, especially the "in general" type, which give a good overall understanding of the subject.*

The screenshots and procedures in this book relate to the Home edition of Windows XP, which will be the system used by most people. However, most of this information is also applicable to the Professional version.

Unfortunately, no major piece of software, XP included, ships without faults (known as bugs). A number of these are detailed in the book, together with solutions. Note that many of the bugs in XP can be fixed by downloading Service Pack 2. Apart from repairing these errors, Service Pack 2 also contains patches (repairs) for the many security issues that have come to light since XP was first released.

Finally, remember that the key to successful troubleshooting, whether it be your PC or your car engine, lies in a considered and logical approach. Establish all the possibilities as far as possible and then use a systematic approach to eliminate them one by one.

# Initial Troubleshooting Steps

There are three ways of tackling a problematic computer system:

1. You can sit back and calmly drink a cup of coffee while you ponder what's just happened (or not happened).

2. You can get extremely agitated, throw caution to the wind and start frantically clicking buttons, adjusting settings, or worse.

3. You can do nothing.

*A panic reaction when your computer goes seriously wrong, will, in all probability, only serve to make matters worse. If you're in this frame of mind, the best policy is to do nothing until you've got a grip on yourself. Then think about what you were doing on the PC prior to the fault appearing. This can often give you a good clue as to the cause of the problem.*

Which of the three reactions is likely to be the best in terms of finding a solution? Well, doing nothing certainly won't help, but it also won't make matters any worse. Going at it like a bull in a china shop might, if you're lucky, result in a quick fix. It might also, though, turn a relatively simple problem into a major one. Spending a few moments in thought before you make your move will undoubtedly increase your chances of making the right move. While it might not be successful, things probably won't be any worse than they were before.

Which approach you take is up to you and may depend on the circumstances. For example, you might need the PC urgently and so decide to take a chance, figuring you've nothing to lose as it's not working anyway. On the other hand, you might be one of those people who don't use their PCs for anything important, and know absolutely nothing about them anyway, and so you might decide to take your PC down to the local repair shop the next time you're in town.

*While it would be unfair to tar all computer help lines with the same brush, it is a fact that the advice given by many of them can actually be anything but helpful. A common problem with help line operators is that when they are asked a question to which they do not have an answer they will often tell the caller that they need to reinstall Windows, when in reality the solution is much simpler.*

For a guaranteed fix, the latter is probably the best course of action. However, probably the majority of users will be unable or unwilling to be without their PC for the length of time this will involve. So what are these people to do?

Many will phone a computer help line, and in many cases will get good advice and soon be back bashing their keyboard. Others, however, won't find a solution this way, and will find the whole experience both frustrating and costly.

*Changing a computer's settings without fully understanding the possible consequences is a major cause of so-called faults. A good piece of advice when considering changing a particular setting, is to investigate the issue on the Internet beforehand. You will find web pages devoted to literally every possible aspect of a computer.*

*Computers are machines, and as with all machines, require a certain amount of maintenance to keep performance levels high. Fortunately, the amount of maintenance needed is relatively low and can mostly be carried out within Windows; de-fragmenting a disk drive is an example. The only physical maintenance a user needs to do is occasionally clear away the dust from the system's circuit boards and fan vents. This needs to be done with care though, to avoid creating problems where none existed before.*

The only other course of action is to do it yourself. Before you start though, consider what we said in the Introduction. Many, if not most, faults are user-induced. So it is quite likely that the problem is due to something that you have recently done on the PC. Therefore, the first thing to do is think back to what you were doing prior to the fault manifesting itself. If you can identify something specific then very often simply "undoing" it will eliminate the problem.

For example, it's extremely likely you have been doing one of the following:

- Downloading from the Internet.

- Installing a peripheral, such as a new scanner.

- Upgrading your PC with new hardware such as a video adapter or hard drive.

- Deleting a program.

- Installing new software.

- Running a program.

- Changing your PC's settings.

- Shutting down your PC incorrectly, either inadvertently or through carelessness.

- Maintenance of some kind.

There are hundreds of thousands of known viruses and more are being developed all the time, the vast majority being spread via the Internet. Many of these viruses can mimic literally any computer fault. So if your PC starts playing up after downloading from the Internet, there is a good chance that it has picked up a virus. Obtain an up-to-date anti-virus program and scan your system.

Installing hardware is a common cause of problems and these are usually conflicts with existing hardware. This type of problem can often be sorted out in the Device Manager.

When uninstalling a program, it is quite common to see a message stating that files about to be deleted might be required by other applications, and offering you a choice as to whether to keep them or not. Always choose to keep these files just in case. Shareware or Freeware programs, available from the Internet or magazine CDs, are often badly written and may not offer you this choice: the files are deleted regardless, leading to subsequent problems.

The system's Registry provides its own backup facility. Use this before making any changes, so that if there is a problem as a result of your changes, you can easily undo them.

Many problems can be resolved by simply rebooting or switching off and then on again. These actions will clear the RAM and reset many settings, which may have become misconfigured: a malfunctioning printer is a typical example.

Often we install a program to try it out and then, having decided we don't want it, we uninstall it. With most programs there is no problem; however, there are some that simply refuse to go quietly. The usual problem is that these programs "borrow" files already on the system and then, when they are uninstalled, take these files with them. Any other programs on the PC that need the files will then not run correctly, if at all. The cure for this is to reinstall the program.

Sometimes, simply running a program will cause problems. It will either have become corrupted or be conflicting with something else on the system. With XP, the result will usually be a frozen PC. Closing the program with the Task Manager (see page 103), rebooting and then trying again should resolve the issue.

It's worth mentioning here that XP is the most stable Windows home operating system yet, and is extremely reliable. Out-and-out crashes are rare.

XP is also a very customizable operating system, which allows the user to make all manner of changes to its default settings. This also applies to much of the systems hardware. However, there are parts of the system where injudicious changes can have adverse effects on the PC's performance. Examples are the BIOS and the Registry. The best policy when experimenting with settings is to make a written note of any changes you make; if there are any subsequent problems then you'll be able to reverse the changes.

There is most definitely a right way and a wrong way to shut down or restart your computer. The right way is to select Start>Restart or Start>Shutdown. The wrong way is to hit the reset button or power off button; this can corrupt any program that might be running, including XP itself. Usually, though, the effects are minor and can be repaired by restarting and then exiting in the proper manner and running Chkdsk (see page 96)

If, for any reason, you have been delving inside the system case, it's quite possible that you have inadvertently loosened or even disconnected something. Retrace your steps, making sure all boards and cables are seated firmly in their sockets.

# Utilize All Available Help

Some applications, video adapter drivers in particular, can cause incompatibility issues with your system; these are often documented in a "Readme" or "Help file" on the CD. Make a point of reading these files, as they can save you a lot of time.

Another frequent cause of problems, particularly when installing a new hardware device, is failure to read the installation instructions. Some devices are very simple to install, but others require a bit more attention. For example, it's not uncommon for some devices or programs to be sold with known bugs that can cause incompatibility issues with other hardware or software. Furthermore, very often these will not be documented in the installation manual, but rather in a file entitled "README" on the CD. Taking a few minutes to read these instructions can save hours of head-scratching and frustration.

All you have to do is right-click on the appropriate disk drive in My Computer and then click Open. This will reveal the contents of the disk.

Another very useful avenue of information, when you are having problems with a specific program or device, is the Internet. Most major applications have forums devoted entirely to issues that other users have experienced with them. Very often you will find the answer there.

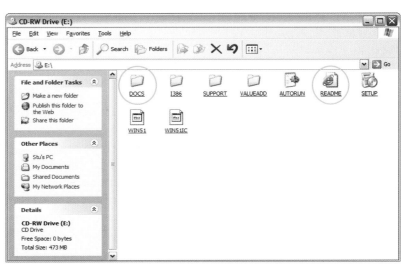

Investigating the contents of an installation disk will often reveal the presence of useful applications. An example is TV tuner software: very often you will find a free video editing and/or video recording program.

This screenshot, taken from the XP installation CD, shows a README file and also a DOCS folder, which contains more information relevant to installing XP. How many people have read them, though?

# Elimination by Substitution

The advice on this page applies particularly when you have problems booting up. Boot problems are usually caused by hardware failures. Often, the only way to establish which device is causing the problem is to physically remove it and then try booting up again. You can do this with sound cards, modems, SCSI adapters and TV tuner cards. Similarly, you can disconnect peripherals such as scanners and printers.

The system will still run without any of these devices. However, mainboards, video adapters, hard drives, monitors and RAM chips need to be replaced, as the system needs these items to run.

Make a point of keeping any working components that you decide to upgrade, particularly the latter items mentioned above. Having a supply of usable hardware components is the most useful troubleshooting aid you can have.

This is what computer repair shops do. Rather than try and find a specific fault on a circuit board or device, they will simply replace it.

## Elimination

Sometimes you'll have a fault with lots of possible causes; it will be a head-scratcher even knowing where to start. It's in situations like this that you'll need to adopt the "sit back and drink a cup of coffee" approach.

What you've got to do is think logically and eliminate as many possibilities as you can. Start by establishing whether the fault is hardware- or software-related. Undo any recent changes made to the system. Remove as much of the system's hardware, such as sound and video adapters, as possible. Disconnect any peripherals, such as printers and scanners. Uninstall any suspect software. In this way you can eliminate many of the possibilities, and gradually the picture will become clearer.

Reboot after every change you make. If, for example, you disconnect all your peripherals in one go and then reboot successfully, you won't know which peripheral was causing the problem.

## Substitution

The easiest way to check a hardware component in your system is to substitute it with one you know to be good. It's also the only way to be absolutely certain that a particular component is either good or bad. A typical example would be when your monitor is dead on boot-up. The most likely causes of this are the monitor itself or the video adapter. But which one? It shouldn't be too difficult to borrow a monitor from a friend or neighbor, or to connect yours to their system. This method can save untold hours of troubleshooting, but does rely on a supply of spare components, which will probably not be readily available. However, many people do upgrade their computers and keep the original parts for just this sort of purpose. A few phone calls to your acquaintances could well unearth what you are looking for.

For this reason it's well worth keeping any working hardware devices you decide to upgrade. Put them somewhere safe, you never know when they might come in handy.

# Troubleshooting Do's & Don'ts

*Neglecting to clean the air vents at the back of the case will eventually lead to overheating. The most likely result of this will be your power supply unit announcing its displeasure with a loud bang and a puff of acrid smelling smoke.*

*Overclocking is something that relatively few people attempt. However, if you do decide to dabble with this, be aware that the results can be disastrous, and, even if it does work, the benefits will be negligible.*

*Software downloaded from the Internet can come with unwelcome attachments. These are usually spyware programs, which monitor your browsing habits and report back. The peer-to-peer or file-sharing networks are also awash with viruses. Always scan software obtained from these sources before running them.*

### Do's

Do keep your computer clean (and by this we don't mean wiping it down occasionally). Every six months or so, open up the system case and remove all the dust that will have accumulated on the circuit boards and particularly in the air vents at the back. The way to do this is with a can of compressed air, available at any computer shop. Simply blow it all away.

Do check that all connections are seated firmly in their sockets before you decide to start replacing boards. If you were fiddling about in the case prior to a fault manifesting itself then also make sure all connections are intact and in the right place.

Do make sure that your hardware drivers are up-to-date. XP is very intolerant of outdated drivers. You can download the latest drivers from the relevant manufacturers' websites.

Do make sure you have grounded yourself before touching any circuit board. (Static electricity in your body can destroy electronic components. RAM chips are particularly vulnerable in this respect.) All you need do is touch the case's metal chassis.

### Don'ts

Don't use a brush to clean dust off circuit boards – this will create static electricity that can render them useless.

Don't plug in keyboards, mice, printers or other devices while the computer is running. Switch the PC off before connecting or disconnecting anything. USB devices are the exception to this rule.

Don't run software applications downloaded from the Internet before scanning them for viruses. This applies particularly to software obtained via file-sharing networks, such as Kazaa.

Don't "cook" your system. Each device you install inside the case will generate heat: overdo it and your components will blow. Most computers will be able to handle a couple of extra devices, but be wary of installing any more than this. If in doubt, install an extra cooling fan. These are readily available from any computer store, and are very easy to fit. Most will come with full instructions.

# XP Troubleshooting Toolkit

You might have got away with it so far, but you can be absolutely certain that one of these days something major will go wrong with your PC. When it does, you will be extremely grateful that you had the good sense to purchase this book and follow the advice on this page. Ideally, you will complete the full kit, which will enable you to deal quickly with any situation. However, if you only get some of the tools, it will still be an advantage when the day comes.

The first thing to put in your toolkit is a complete backup of your operating system, settings, installed software and data. A good method of doing this is explained on pages 44–45. If your problem isn't hardware-related, this will enable you to be up and running again in no time.

Secondly, you will need your XP installation CD, together with the serial number. If it's an upgrade version, you will also need the CD of your previous version of Windows.

Thirdly, you need to familiarize yourself with XP's main troubleshooting tools: Startup Options, System Configuration Utility, and Device Manager.

Fourthly, into your toolkit you will place a spare monitor, video adapter, hard drive, RAM chip and a mainboard. Obviously, most people aren't going to go out and buy these items (which are basically a computer system in themselves), but if you do happen to possess any, put them in.

Lastly, you will put this book into the toolkit for handy reference.

Even if you ignore the fourth step, you will still be able to resolve any startup problem. Boot problems could well need some of the hardware listed above, but fortunately these are less common.

If you want to be able to deal with major problems as and when they arise, you'll find that a little effort now, when you've got the time, will save a lot of effort and grief later on when perhaps you haven't got the time.

# XP Setup Troubleshooting

Given an adequately specified computer, setting up XP is a relatively straightforward process. Usually, all you have to do is sit there drinking coffee and clicking OK periodically.

However, there are things that can go wrong, and this chapter will explain the more common problems and what to do about them.

There are also a few simple steps that every user should take before an XP installation, which will help ensure a problem-free setup.

## Covers

Chapter Two

# Can Your System Handle XP?

Windows XP is a complicated and powerful piece of software, much more so than its predecessors: Windows 95, 98, NT, Me and 2000.

*Users of Windows 95 or earlier will find there is no upgrade path to XP; a new installation will be required. Windows 98, 98SE, and Me users can upgrade to either XP Home or Professional versions. Windows NT 4.0, Windows 2000 and XP Home users can upgrade to XP Professional, but not to XP Home.*

Each version has introduced new features and technology designed to improve and further the operating systems capabilities. However, all this comes at a price – namely the system resources or requirements needed to run it. This is particularly so with XP.

Therefore, if you are having trouble installing XP, take a look at what your system should have.

Microsoft's <u>recommended</u> system requirements are:

* Processor speed of 300 MHz.

* 128 MB of RAM.

* 1.5 GB available hard disk space.

* SuperVGA (800 x 600) resolution video adapter and monitor.

*The important figures to note are those for CPU speed and RAM capacity. These are critical, and, if your system is lacking in either, XP will not be an enjoyable experience.*

The two important requirements are the processor speed and RAM. The <u>minimum</u> requirements for these are:

* Processor speed of 233 MHz.

* 64 MB of RAM (may limit performance and some features).

Many people who have been running Windows 95, 98 or Me on their computers, upgrade to XP with the happy assumption that this will work equally as well. Others will have read the recommended system requirements on the box, see that their system comes close, and so buy it.

*To find out your system's specifications, do the following: Go to Start, All Programs, Accessories, System Tools and finally System Information. The utility will open at the System Summary page, which will list your system's specs.*

*Alternatively, right-click My Computer and click Properties. At the bottom of the dialog box, you will see your CPU and RAM specifications.*

However, as with all manufacturer's claims, these figures need to be taken with a large pinch of salt. Yes, XP may run, but its performance could well be far short of what the user expects.

This issue of system requirements can have major effects on the installation of XP, as we shall see in this chapter.

# Problems with New Installations

*If you carry out a new installation by formatting your hard drive, you will lose all your data. There may be nothing there you want to keep, but more likely there will be. In this case, you need to make a backup of your data before you format. The usual mediums for this are writable CDs or a second hard drive.*

*While on this subject, there are some excellent backup utilities on the market, such as Norton Ghost and PowerQuest's Drive Image. These utilities will enable you to make a complete or selective backup of your entire system.*

*In the event of a disaster, they make restoring your system a simple matter.*

*XP supplies a Files & Settings Transfer Wizard, which will enable you to transfer your original system settings. You will find this by clicking Perform Additional Tasks on the first screen of the XP installation routine – see page 182.*

*Don't forget to run the "Check System Compatibility" check from the installation CD. Alternatively, check out the Microsoft website. This will alert you to any potential problems.*

One of the most frequently asked questions is whether it is possible to do a new installation using an upgrade version of XP. The answer to this is, Yes. At some point during the setup procedure, however, Windows XP will ask you to insert your qualifying media to ensure that you are eligible. The media must be a retail Windows 95, 98, 98 Second Edition, Millennium Edition, NT 4.0 or 2000 CD-ROM, be it an upgrade or full version. Note that the rescue disks provided by PC manufacturers with computers that have XP preinstalled are not considered as qualifying operating systems and will not be accepted.

If you already have an existing installation of XP, the first thing you will see is an option to repair the installation by pressing R on the keyboard. Do not select this.

The next screen will list all the existing partitions for each hard disk on the system. Use the arrow keys to choose which drive or partition you are going to use for the new installation. Then press the Enter key, and you will see the format screen.

The format procedure wipes the drive/partition clean of all data, including any potential issues that might cause problems with the installation: viruses, hardware conflicts, etc. For this reason, a new installation is much more likely to succeed than an upgrade.

<u>IMPORTANT</u>: Do not format your hard disk before making a backup of any data you wish to keep. If you want to keep the settings from your previous Windows installation, run the Files and Settings Transfer wizard – see page 182.

Because the format procedure clears the hard drive, a new installation is extremely unlikely to be anything other than successful. About the only thing that might cause problems is system hardware. XP does have compatibility issues with certain hardware devices, and, if you happen to have one of these in your system, you might well find that the installation will grind to a halt.

If this happens, the thing to do is to switch off the PC and remove as much of your hardware as you can. Sound, network and SCSI cards can all be taken out. Also, unplug any USB devices, with the exception of your mouse and keyboard. If this solves the problem

At the risk of stating the obvious, if you disconnect your USB keyboard or mouse, you'll lose control of your computer.

Previous versions of Windows needed a boot floppy disk for installation. This required the floppy disk drive to be configured as the first boot device.

XP, however, is supplied on a bootable CD. Therefore the CD-ROM drive must be configured as the first boot device if you are installing to a new hard disk drive.

The exact layouts of BIOS setup programs vary slightly according to the manufacturer. However, they are all basically the same, so you should encounter no problem finding your way around.

Remember to save your changes when you exit the BIOS, otherwise the settings will revert back to their original values.

then reinstall the devices one by one, restarting each time, until you have located the troublemaker.

If Setup still fails, you might find your system's BIOS needs updating. This is only likely though if you have an old system (in which case you might find that XP isn't the best operating system for you). Either upgrade the BIOS or get a modern system.

If you are installing to a new hard drive you might well see a message saying "No operating system was found" or similar. XP's setup stops at this point. This is because the BIOS is looking in the wrong drive for the installation disk. Fix this as follows:

1  Reboot and go into the BIOS setup program (see page 51). Use the arrow keys to select Advanced BIOS Features and then scroll down to First Boot Device.

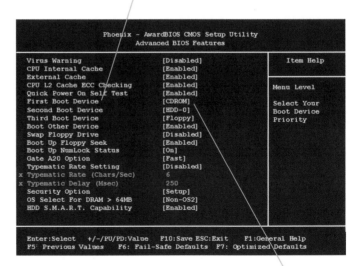

2  Then use the Page Up/Page Down keys on your keyboard to select CD-ROM. Save your changes and exit the BIOS. Reboot, and this time you will see a message at the bottom of the second boot-up screen saying "Press any key to boot from CD." Do so, and XP's installation routine will begin.

# Problems with Upgrading

*Before doing an upgrade to XP, make sure you do the following:*

1) *Ensure your hard drive is in good order by running Scandisk and Disk Defragmenter – hard drive problems can halt the installation.*

2) *Check your system for viruses. Having done that, uninstall the anti-virus program. These are notorious for causing installation problems.*

3) *Disable any programs that run in the background and suddenly activate, such as screensavers and utility programs.*

4) *Remove all programs in the Startup folder.*

5) *Make sure your hardware drivers are XP-compatible. This applies particularly to network adapters, video adapters, modems and hard drive controllers.*

6) *Run the "Check System Compatibility" check from the installation CD. Alternatively, check out the Microsoft website.*

7) *Disconnect peripherals such as scanners and printers – USB devices in particular.*

*If your system is three or more years old, it would be a good idea to upgrade it. See page 33 for details on how to upgrade a BIOS.*

You've decided to take the upgrade option. That's fine as long as you're aware that you are much more likely to have problems, as the setup procedure now has to contend with adjusting itself to all your original settings and applications. Let's start with a common problem.

### XP Takes Ages to Install

The answer to this is simple – your system's CPU and RAM are not up to the job, and they're struggling with the demands XP is making of them. Right-click My Computer (when you eventually get XP running) and then click Properties. At the bottom of the dialog box you will see your CPU speed and installed RAM. If the CPU speed is less than 233 MHz or RAM is 64 MB or less, then you must upgrade them. You are also quite likely to see XP just keep rebooting in a continuous cycle, or simply stop at the Welcome screen (very frustrating). If your system is properly specified, XP's installation routine should take no more than 20 to 30 minutes.

### File Copy Error During Setup

You receive the following message (or something similar):

"Setup cannot copy the file ......... Press X to retry, Y to abort."

The first thing to check is that the XP CD is clean and free of scratches.

You might have two or more CD-ROM drives on your system. If so, XP could be looking in the wrong drive for the installation files. Disable or disconnect the other drives.

If you have a Memory Manager installed on your system, uninstall it. XP is excellent at managing a PC's memory, but previous versions were less so; this spawned a multitude of programs that optimized RAM. However, with XP they are completely unnecessary, and will cause more problems than they prevent.

### Computer Stops Responding

Wait 15 minutes before restarting the installation. Sometimes Setup will resume after a long period of inactivity. On the second attempt, if Setup advances further before stopping again, restart and keep restarting and see if the installation manages to complete.

*XP's underlying architecture is radically different from 95, 98 and Me. This means that many hardware drivers that worked with these systems will not be compatible with XP. These drivers can cause problems during the hardware detection stage of the XP installation routine. You are well advised to run the Check System Compatibility option, which you will see at the bottom of the installation routine's opening screen.*

*Users upgrading from Windows 95 need to type SYSEDIT in the Start menu Run box. This will open the System Configuration Editor, which is essentially the same as the System Configuration Utility found in later versions of Windows.*

*If you have a separate video adapter in your system, and your mainboard supports onboard video, then enable it and remove the video adapter as well. Otherwise you'll have to leave it in. (With no video you'll have a blank display.) Video adapters are one of the most common causes of setup problems, so if you can remove it as described above, do so.*

If it doesn't, you have a compatibility or configuration problem with an item of hardware or software. Check out the software issue by restarting and choosing the option to "Cancel Windows XP Setup." Then reboot into your original operating system (95, 98, Me, etc.) and uninstall any anti-virus software. Remove all programs from the Start Menu folder, disable any screensaver and defragment your drive. Reboot and try again.

If Setup still fails then revert back to your original version of Windows again, and this time run the System Configuration Utility by typing MSCONFIG into the Run box on the Start Menu (Windows 95 users must type SYSEDIT, which will open the System Configuration Editor).

Locate the General tab, click Selective Startup and then clear all the checkboxes. Click OK and then restart the PC when prompted to do so. See pages 39 and 41 for more details on this procedure.

What you are doing here is performing what is known as a "clean boot," which basically means starting the PC in a "bare bones" state. Under normal circumstances, when you start your computer it loads many files and programs to customize the operating environment. A clean boot eliminates these optional features and loads only those files and programs that are absolutely essential, thus cutting out many potential problems.

Retry the XP installation. If it works this time then go back to the System Configuration Utility and one by one recheck the items under Selective Startup, rebooting after each change, until you have located the problem.

If you are still having problems, or can't revert back to your original setup, then you need to investigate your hardware. Remove all PCI cards such as network cards, sound cards and modems. Disconnect all USB devices (apart from the mouse and keyboard) and any peripherals such as scanners and printers.

Still no joy! Something in your existing setup is preventing XP from installing, but you can't isolate it. The only sensible option now is to eradicate everything. This means a new installation, as described on pages 56–57. If this fails as well then an item of hardware you haven't removed is to blame.

# Dual Booting – Ground Rules

With XP's dual boot facility, Microsoft have for the first time given users the opportunity to run two or more operating systems on the same computer without the need for third-party software.

*If you have only one hard drive in your system then you will need to partition it. The simplest way to do this is with a partition utility such as Powerquest's Partition Magic. However, if you don't have this, then XP supplies you with all the tools you need, although it will be a more long-winded process.*

However, before you attempt to do this, there are a few ground rules you ought to familiarize yourself with.

Each operating system must be installed to a separate hard drive. However, even if you have only one drive, you can still dual boot; in this case you must split your drive to create two or more partitions, each of which will appear as a separate drive to Windows. See the margin note and also pages 56–57.

There are also limitations on which combination of Windows versions you can dual boot with XP. The main one concerns Windows 95, 98 and Me: you can have only one of these systems dual booting with XP.

Non-Microsoft operating systems will not work with XP's boot manager.

*In a dual/ multiboot setup, Windows will, by default, boot to the first listed operating system in the boot options screen.*

*Because XP has to be installed last in the dual/multiboot setup, this means it will be the last operating system in the boot options, i.e. not the default.*

*However, many users will want XP to be the default operating system. The way to configure this is as follows:*

*Boot into XP and go to Start, Control Panel & System. Click the Advanced tab and under Startup and Recovery, click Settings. At the top of the new dialog box, under System Startup, you will see the list of operating systems. Using the drop-down box, select Windows XP, and it will then be the default system.*

The table below shows possible dual boot configurations:

- MS-DOS.
- Windows 95 or Windows 98 or Windows Me.
- Windows NT.
- Windows 2000.
- Windows XP (Home or Professional).

Having decided which systems you wish to install, the next thing you must do is install them in the correct order.

The rule is that you install your chosen systems in order of age, beginning with the oldest. XP (either Home or Pro) is the system you install last. An example setup is shown below:

- Windows 98 – installed first on Drive C.
- Windows 2000 – installed second on Drive D.
- Windows XP – installed last on Drive E.

If you follow the above rules then you will be able to successfully dual boot with XP. Do it any other way and you will find it an extremely frustrating experience.

# Dual Booting – Problems

*Install all your applications to a common folder by installing them on one OS, then booting the other OSes and reinstalling the applications into the same folder. Very often they will work on all the operating systems without the need to install separate copies. This doesn't always work though, and depends on your particular setup. It's worth a try nevertheless.*

*If you want all your drives/ partitions to be available when using Windows 95, 98 or Me in a dual boot environment with XP, then format all the drives/partitions with the FAT file system.*

*XP's boot manager won't let you run more than one version of Windows 95, 98 or Me. However, if this is what you really want to do, then you need a more advanced boot manager such as PowerQuest's Boot Magic. As this is a third-party utility though, you will need to pay for it.*

*Third-party disk managers, such as Seagate's Disk Manager, which are often used to achieve a large hard drive's full capacity (see page 58), can play havoc with a dual boot system. If you try this, backup your data first.*

## You Cannot Boot to XP

When you boot your new dual boot setup, you cannot see an option allowing you to boot XP. Assuming a Windows 98/XP setup as an example, you can boot to only Windows 98.

This is because you installed Windows 98 last, instead of first as you should have done. The result is that Windows 98 has overwritten XP's boot sector, which contains its startup files.

The solution is to run XP's setup routine again. Setup will detect the existing XP installation and ask if you want to repair it. Press "R" and XP will reinstall itself. As it is now the last system to be installed, when you reboot you will see the XP boot option.

Sometimes you will see the XP boot option but it won't work – all you get are error messages. This can happen after running Windows 95 or 98 for the first time, which is known to occasionally reconfigure hardware settings, which in turn can cause device conflicts. Again, the solution is to reinstall XP.

## XP's Drive/Partition Is Not Visible

When running Windows 95, 98 or Me, you can't see the drive or partition on which XP is installed. However, when running XP you can see the drive on which 95/98/Me is installed. The cause of this is that XP's drive has been formatted with the NTFS file system (which Windows 95/98/Me cannot read, whereas XP can read any Windows file system).

The only solution is to convert XP's NTFS drive/partition to FAT, which 95/98/Me will be able to read. The simplest way is with a partition utility such as Partition Magic, which will do the conversion without destroying the XP installation. Otherwise, you will have to reformat the XP drive/partition with the XP CD using the FAT option and then install XP again.

## Programs Don't Work with Dual Boot

You've set up a dual boot system and now programs in one or both of the systems don't work. Managing a dual boot system is a tricky operation and sometimes XP will get it wrong. The only solution is to reinstall the affected programs.

# Hardware Boot-up Troubleshooting

The term "boot-up" relates to what happens in a computer between hitting the On switch and the Windows Desktop appearing on the display.

The boot procedure has two distinct stages – checking & initializing the system's hardware and then loading the operating system.

This chapter investigates the first of these stages – hardware.

## Covers

Chapter Three

# Boot-up Fails to Start

You've switched on and discovered that all is not well. Instead of seeing the black boot-up screens with incomprehensible white text, all you see is a black screen. No matter how many times you restart the PC, the result is the same.

*Absolutely the first thing to check when your PC appears to be "dead" is the power supply. Don't forget to check the external (mains) power supply as well.*

### Troubleshooting The Power Supply

The first thing to establish is whether you have power available to your PC. This principle applies to any item of electronic or electrical equipment, not just computers, and in this case is easily established by observation.

Are the LEDs (lights) on the system case lit and is the power supply fan running? Do you see any lights on your keyboard? If the answer to any of these questions is yes, then the system's power supply is operational.

*The easiest way to establish that your power supply unit is operational is to check that the fan is working and that the keyboard lights are on.*

If the answer is no, then check the following:

1   Is there power at the wall socket? Plug another appliance into it; if that works then the socket is OK.

2   Are you using a surge suppressor, cable extension or some similar device? If so, try removing or bypassing it and see if that cures the problem.

3   Next, check the PC's power cable. Try substituting it with your electric kettle cable; these are often the same type.

4   Many PCs also have an on/off switch at the top rear of the case. Check that this isn't in the off position.

If none of these is causing the problem, then the PC's power supply unit is defective and will need replacing.

However, if your power supply is functioning, then the problem is reduced to one of three potential issues: the monitor, the mainboard or the video adapter is faulty.

# Troubleshooting the Monitor

The first of these possibilities to rule out is the monitor.

*At the risk of stating the obvious, do check that the monitor's Brightness and/or Contrast control hasn't been turned right down inadvertently. Also, make sure the power cable is firmly plugged in.*

Most modern monitors display a message or splash screen of some sort when switched on, to indicate they are working. The monitor must be disconnected from the computer for this to work.

Switch both monitor and computer off and then disconnect the cable from the video socket. If you're not sure which this is then simply follow the cable from the monitor to where it plugs in at the rear of the system case.

Switch the monitor back on (not the computer) and you should now see a message similar to the one below.

*Try turning the Brightness control right up as far as it will go. If the screen goes gray and you see lines on the screen, this indicates that the problem is likely to be a faulty video adapter or video cable, with a lesser possibility of a faulty monitor.*

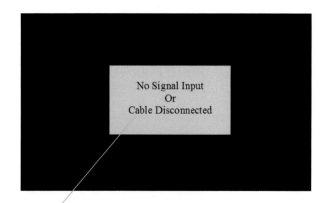

This indicates that the monitor is working, as is its power supply.

*Monitors carry high voltages, which can be lethal. These voltages will remain until discharged – make sure they aren't discharged through you! It's obviously possible to open up a dud monitor and locate a specific fault, assuming you have the knowledge and requisite test equipment, but if you don't, quite apart from wasting your time and invalidating any existing warranty, you'll also quite literally be risking your life. Always take a defective monitor to a repair shop.*

If you don't see a message and the monitor lights are off, then either the monitor itself is faulty or it's not getting any power. Check the power supply, cable and connections. If these are OK then the monitor must be faulty.

If you want to be absolutely sure before going out and buying a new one then the only conclusive test is to either substitute it with one known to be good or connect it to a different system.

Once you have eliminated the monitor, the next thing to check is the mainboard. This takes us into the realm of beep codes.

# Beep Codes

The procedure for eliminating the mainboard and the video adapter is essentially the same – what you must do is to listen to the PC and see if it is telling you anything in the form of unusual noises. If it is, you will hear an irregular pattern of beeps, known as beep codes, which indicate specific faults.

If you are getting beep codes then you will need to know what the various codes mean. However, the different BIOS chip manufacturers all use different codes, so first you must find out who the maker of your chip is. This information should be in your computer documentation. If it isn't, though, you can get it from the mainboard.

*The BIOS chip has a built-in diagnostic system, which alerts you to any problems it encounters during boot-up. It does this in two ways – a series of coded beeps if the problem occurs before the video system has initialized, or a text error message if the fault comes after.*

To do this you will have to open up the system case and locate the BIOS chip on the mainboard. There will be a sticker on top of the chip with the name of the manufacturer. The chip is often, but not always, located at the bottom-left side of the mainboard.

*You may find it difficult to locate the BIOS chip, as it may be obscured from view by the PCI cards plugged into the mainboard. It might be necessary to remove some or all of these.*

*This isn't difficult to do – just remember to ground yourself beforehand. Also, if possible, hold the cards by the edges – try not to touch the components.*

BIOS Chip – in this example, it's an AWARD BIOS

The three main BIOS manufacturers are AWARD, AMI and PHOENIX. For details of these manufacturers' beep codes, refer to the list at the end of this chapter.

# Troubleshooting the Mainboard

*You should hear one beep when the PC is switched on. This is normal and indicates everything is as it should be.*

*The mainboard is the only system component that is not easy to replace. If in any doubt, take the computer to a repair shop.*

*Before condemning a mainboard, it's worth reseating the CPU and RAM chips. Then remove as much system hardware as possible before rebooting. It sometimes does the trick.*

*No beeps at all, particularly if combined with no keyboard lights, indicates a definite mainboard failure. The only conclusive test of a mainboard is replacement with one known to be good.*

The mainboard is literally the heart of a computer system, and as such is a complex piece of circuitry. Every single part of a PC is connected to this board.

There are several different beep codes relating to faults with the mainboard itself and specific mainboard components such as RAM and the CPU. These latter faults can often be repaired by replacing or reseating the relevant chips, and aren't necessarily too big a disaster.

However, there is always the possibility of not getting any beeps at all, which almost always indicates an outright failure of the mainboard. You will usually find that the keyboard lights are not working either. In this case, you'll just have to bite the bullet and get the mainboard replaced.

The following beep codes indicate major mainboard problems, and are the ones most likely to be heard.

## AWARD

No beeps – mainboard fault.
Any other sequence – memory fault.

## AMI

No beeps – mainboard fault.
Two to four beeps – memory fault.
Five beeps – CPU failure.
Six beeps – mainboard fault.
Seven beeps – CPU failure.
Nine to eleven beeps – mainboard fault.

## PHOENIX

Phoenix codes are emitted in a sequence of three beeps with each set being separated by a brief pause.

1-1-2 to 1-1-4 – mainboard fault.
1-2-1 to 1-2-3 – mainboard fault.
1-3-3 to 1-3-4 – mainboard failure.
1-4-2 – memory fault.

For a full list of beep codes see page 34.

# Troubleshooting the Video Adapter

The next issue to investigate is the video adapter. This is the device most likely to prevent a PC booting. Unfortunately, for most users, troubleshooting options for a video adapter are limited to checking that the card is firmly seated in its socket. Unless you have another card known to be good, which you can substitute, there is little else you can do. Likely beep code errors are:

## AWARD

One long, one short beep – video system failure.

## AMI

Eight beeps – video system failure.

## PHOENIX

3-3-4 – video system failure.

If there are no abnormal beep codes then it could be that the video adapter is conflicting with another hardware device. To eliminate this possibility, one by one, physically remove every device in the system, restarting each time and seeing if the PC boots. If and when it does, then the last device removed will be the culprit. Once back in Windows, you can troubleshoot the issue in the Device Manager. Reinstalling the device's driver will usually resolve the problem.

Another possibility is that a new video adapter has been installed on a PC that was previously using an onboard video system built into the mainboard. For the new video adapter to work, the onboard video may need to be disabled, otherwise the two might conflict, with the result that neither works. On older systems, there will usually be a jumper setting on the mainboard that must be altered. With newer systems, the video card should automatically override the onboard video; if not, the change will be made in the BIOS setup program.

The details of these procedures will be in the computer's documentation. If you've lost it, you may have to borrow a friend's PC to download a copy from the manufacturer's website.

# Boot-up Starts But Fails to Complete

The BIOS is a chip situated on the mainboard that contains all the initialization routines required to boot the computer and then load the operating system.

Instructions on how to access the BIOS setup program will be seen on the boot screen. Typically, it will read "Press ..... key to enter setup." Often it is the Delete key.

This situation is almost always accompanied by a text error message (known as a Boot Time Error Message), which indicates that there is at least output from the video system and that the mainboard is probably OK. (For an error message to be displayed, the video system must be working.)

The thing to do is to observe what message is on the screen when the boot procedure stops. In many cases they are self-explanatory – such as "Invalid system disk" or "Disk error" when you boot up with a floppy disk inserted in the floppy disk drive. Sometimes though, they can be more cryptic, but will often give some indication of where the problem lies.

If the boot screen flashes by before you have time to read it, you can pause it by pressing the Pause key on the keyboard. Press the Enter key to resume the boot-up.

```
Verifying DMI Pool Data...
Boot From CD:

Disk Boot Failure, Insert System Disk and Press Enter
```

If you see the error message opposite, but the message stops at "Verifying DMI Pool Data," the meaning will be the same – a hard disk problem.

This is a common XP error message; very often the fault can be resolved by switching off the computer, removing the system case cover, and reseating the hard disk IDE cable connections. See page 53.

In the above example, the boot procedure has stopped with a disk boot error message. This message indicates the hard drive on which the operating system is installed has failed. This could be a problem with the drive itself, its connections, or a configuration issue.

These error messages are produced by the BIOS, as it is responsible for the boot procedure functions. However, there are other error messages, known as Run Time Error Messages, which are specific to the operating system.

As there so many different things that can prevent a successful boot, the first step is to isolate the problem. This is done by interpreting these error messages and noting at which stage of the boot procedure the boot-up stops.

Let's see what should be happening when you switch on your computer.

*Plug & Play is a uniform standard adopted by all the major computer manufacturers. It allows a device to be installed to a system as painlessly as possible – the operating system will see that new hardware has been added to the system and automatically configure the device so that it works properly and doesn't interfere with other devices already on the system.*

*Prior to the advent of Plug & Play, all this had be done manually by the user.*

## Boot Procedure

The first thing you should see on boot-up is the BIOS message showing details of the video system, which indicates that it is working. (In some systems you might not see this message.) If boot-up stops at this point then the problem is most likely to be with the video system.

Next, you will see details of your BIOS chip. Details of which key to hit in order to enter the BIOS setup program will be shown at the bottom of the screen.

The BIOS will now perform the memory test. If it doesn't, or hangs at this stage, there is a problem with your system's RAM.

Next comes detection of IDE devices, such as hard drives and CD-ROM/DVD/Floppy drives. Problems at this stage will usually result in error messages saying the system is having trouble identifying one or more of the IDE devices. This indicates a problem with the device itself or its configuration.

The BIOS will now attempt to identify any Plug & Play devices in the system. A hang-up here is usually caused by an expansion card such as a modem or sound card. The card could be faulty or causing a resource conflict. Troubleshoot by unplugging all the cards in turn and restarting each time.

You should now see a system configuration summary detailing all the hardware the BIOS has found in the system. Note that on modern well-specified computer systems, the system configuration screen, which is the second boot screen, will load so fast you probably won't even see it. Unless there is a problem, that is, in which case you will. If you want to see it, press the Pause key to pause it.

The BIOS will now look in your hard drive for the operating system. This will be indicated by lights and physical activity in the drive. Any failure at this stage indicates problems with the drive – refer to the Hard Drive troubleshooter.

If the operating system loads, or begins to load, then the hardware part of the boot procedure has been successful.

# Upgrading a System BIOS

*BIOS updates are available from numerous websites. Identifying the correct one for your system, however, can be a tricky process.*

*To do it, you will need the manufacturers and model numbers of both your BIOS chip and mainboard. Armed with this information, you then need to visit the website of your mainboard's manufacturer, where you should be able to find and download the appropriate update.*

*Another way to do this is via a specialist BIOS update website. Typically, these sites will run an identification utility, which will automatically extract all the relevant information from your system. This will then be presented to you in the form of a summary and a recommended BIOS update. However, this type of site will require that cash changes hands before the update is available. Usually, it will be emailed to you.*

*Some mainboard manufacturers now have available from their websites an automatic BIOS upgrade utility. All you have to do is click a button; the upgrade is then downloaded and installed without you having to leave Windows.*

Firstly, when is it necessary to do this? In almost all cases the answer is when you are trying to run software or a device that uses advanced technology on an outdated computer system.

A typical example is the modern breed of hard drive, which can have capacities of 250 GB and more. Older BIOSes will typically "see" only 32 GB, and the vast majority of the disk space will be unusable. Upgrading the BIOS will sometimes fix this issue.

With regard to software, Windows XP is a classic example, as it employs various technologies that must be supported by the BIOS before they will function. Again, upgrading is the answer.

So, how is it done? On anything other than really old systems, where the BIOS chip must be physically removed and then replaced with a new one, the answer is to "Flash" it. What this basically means is that existing instructions in the BIOS are overwritten with an updated version.

To do it you need two things:

- The BIOS update, which comes in the form of a small file.

- A Flash program, which carries out the flash operation. An example is shown below.

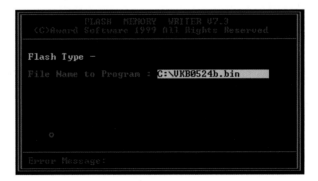

Run the Flash program and then type in the location of the BIOS update file. Then press Enter. The program will prompt you first to back up the existing BIOS and then to perform the update. Reboot and you're done.

# Manufacturers' Beep Codes

The main suppliers of BIOS chips are Award, AMI and Phoenix.

## AWARD

No beeps – mainboard fault.
One beep – normal.
One long, one short beep – video system fault.
One long, then three short beeps – video system fault.
Any other sequence – memory fault.

## AMI

No beeps – mainboard fault.
One beep – normal.
Two to four beeps – memory fault.
Five beeps – CPU fault.
Six beeps – mainboard fault.
Seven beeps – CPU fault.
Eight beeps – video system fault.
Nine to eleven beeps – mainboard fault.

## PHOENIX

1-1-2 – mainboard fault.
1-1-3 – mainboard fault.
1-1-4 – mainboard fault.
1-2-1 – mainboard fault.
1-2-2 – mainboard fault.
1-2-3 – mainboard fault.
1-3-1 – mainboard fault.
1-3-2 – mainboard fault.
1-3-3 – mainboard fault.
1-3-4 – mainboard fault.
1-4-1 – mainboard fault.
1-4-2 – memory fault.
3-2-4 – mainboard fault.
3-3-4 – video system fault.
4-2-1 – mainboard fault.
4-2-2 – mainboard fault.
4-2-3 – mainboard fault.
4-3-1 – mainboard fault.
4-3-2 – mainboard fault.
4-3-3 – mainboard fault.
4-3-4 – mainboard fault.

*The full list of beep codes for Phoenix is very long and, due to space restrictions, we have only been able to list the codes most likely to be heard. The complete list is readily available from many websites – www.webopedia.com, for example.*

*Phoenix uses sequences of beeps to indicate problems. The "-" between each number indicates a pause between each beep sequence. For example, 1-2-3 indicates one beep followed by a pause, two beeps followed by a pause, and three beeps.*

*Award uses the fewest beep codes of any of the BIOS manufacturers. They prefer to display a message that describes the error. The only time you will get any beeps is if the video system fails or there is a RAM problem.*

# Startup/Shutdown Troubleshooting

Assuming the hardware boot-up stage has gone as it should, you are still only halfway to getting your PC operational.

This chapter covers problems likely to be experienced during the software stage of the boot procedure. This involves getting XP running, and it's at this point that most boot problems are encountered.

Having got XP running, you may then find you have problems shutting it down. Again, we'll see how to resolve issues of this type.

## Covers

Chapter Four

# XP Refuses to Start

The hardware detection and configuration stage of the boot procedure has completed and the BIOS now looks for the operating system in the computer's drives.

*Many problems are induced by users simply not exiting XP in the correct way. Sometimes it's unavoidable, but wherever possible exit correctly.*

Sometimes, however, for whatever reason, XP just won't start. You may get an error message, you may see almost nothing at all – just the cursor flickering uselessly at the top or bottom of a black screen – or XP may just keep rebooting. No matter how many times you try, the result is the same.

In this situation, remember there is often a simple solution. For example, there is a possibility that the last time you exited Windows, you didn't do it properly (Start>Shutdown or Start>Restart). Instead, you may have done one of the following:

- Hit the PC's reset button.

*A reboot will often solve any number of computer faults that crop up from time to time.*

*A typical example is a printer that refuses to print, or seems to have developed a mind of its own, churning out reams and reams of unrequested stuff. A reboot will usually reset the printer's settings, thus resolving the issue.*

- Switched the computer off with the on/off button while XP was running.

- Crashed the computer.

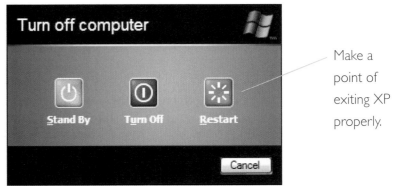

Make a point of exiting XP properly.

With any of these "exits" you run the risk of corrupting XP's startup files, with the result that XP will refuse to load on restart. Simply exiting XP properly can often repair this type of fault. On restart, Chkdsk should automatically run and repair any damaged files. Therefore, this is the first thing to try.

The question is, how can you switch off correctly if you can't get into XP in the first place?

# Troubleshooting XP in Safe Mode

*Safe Mode is a method of loading Windows when there is a critical problem interfering with the normal operation of Windows. Safe Mode allows the user to troubleshoot the operating system to determine the cause of the problem. For example, adding new software or hardware to the system can cause conflicts with existing programs and hardware. In Safe Mode, the only programs that are loaded are the operating system and drivers for the mouse, keyboard and video system. The main portion of the Registry is not loaded.*

*Because Safe Mode loads only a minimal set of drivers, a computer will not perform as normal. Don't expect to be running all your applications and browsing the Internet.*

*When in Safe Mode, the computer will be slow, and many applications will not work at all. Safe Mode is for troubleshooting purposes only.*

The answer is to start XP in Safe Mode. This is Windows's troubleshooting mode and is designed to get XP going if at all possible. Safe Mode works by bypassing the normal Windows configuration, instead loading a minimum set of basic drivers. This eliminates a number of issues that might prevent XP from starting, and will often get you back into XP, from where you can find and fix the problem.

To do it, reboot and keep tapping the F8 key until you see the Windows Advanced Options menu.

```
Windows Advanced Options Menu
Please select An Option

Safe Mode
Safe Mode With Networking
Safe Mode With Command Prompt

Enable Boot Logging
Enable VGA Mode
Last Known Good Configuration (Yout Most Recent Settings That Worked)
Directory Services Restore Mode (Windows Domain Controllers Only)

Start Windows Normally
Reboot
Return To OS Choices Menu

Use the up and down arrow keys to move the highlight to your choice
```

Use the arrow keys to select Safe Mode, and then hit Enter.

With a bit of luck, XP will now start. It will take longer than normal, so give it time. You will also find that while in Safe Mode, XP will run a lot slower and many of its functions will be disabled. However, you will be able to access XP's various troubleshooting utilities, which will help you resolve many of the issues that prevent XP from starting normally.

At the moment though, all we want to do is exit XP correctly and see if that solves the problem. So, assuming XP does start in Safe Mode, go to Start, Turn off Computer and click Restart.

If XP now starts normally then your problem is solved. If it doesn't, go to the next page. If XP won't start in Safe Mode either, its startup files are severely damaged. The simplest option here is to repair it as described on page 40.

# Fixing XP With System Restore

If XP still won't run, we need to dig deeper. Before we do though, there is an easy option that just might do the trick and so save a lot of time and effort.

XP provides a utility called System Restore, which works by creating a backup of your system when changes, such as installations of new hardware and software, are made to it. In the event of problems, the PC can be restored to one of these backups.

Reboot into Safe Mode and, when back in XP, go to Start, All Programs, Accessories, System Tools and System Restore.

Choose a Restore Point created at an earlier date. Then click Next.

Your system will now be restored to exactly how it was when the Restore Point selected was made.

Note that when you use System Restore, although you won't lose any of your data, all programs and system settings you have installed/changed since the restore date will be lost.

If XP still won't run after doing this, then we need to use another of its troubleshooting utilities.

# System Configuration Utility

*One of the tools included with Windows XP is the System Configuration Utility. This is a diagnostic program that provides you with a simple and effective way of troubleshooting system issues by the process of elimination. The main element that it controls is the boot environment; it allows you to control which drivers, services, startup programs, system.ini and win.ini files are loaded during boot-up. You can control the elements as a group or individually – the intention being that the tool will ultimately allow you to isolate a system boot problem.*

Boot XP into Safe Mode and then click Start, Run. In the Run box type MSCONFIG. Hit Enter. The System Configuration Utility will now open. Click the General tab.

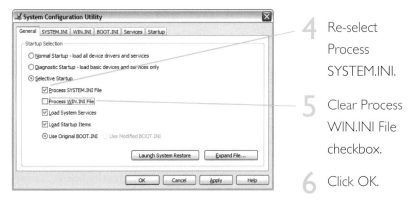

1 Click Selective Startup.

2 Clear the Process SYSTEM.INI File checkbox.

3 Click OK.

The computer will reboot. If XP now starts normally, go to page 41. If it doesn't, reboot into Safe Mode again and return to the System Configuration Utility as described above.

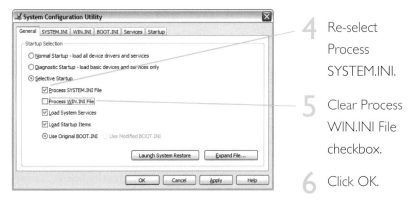

4 Re-select Process SYSTEM.INI.

5 Clear Process WIN.INI File checkbox.

6 Click OK.

*The Win.ini file is the system file that was used to start programs in previous versions of Windows. While it is not required by Windows XP itself (XP keeps these settings in the registry), many third-party applications still use it. Thus, to provide backward compatibility with these applications, it is included in XP.*

*The System.ini file is used to initialize system settings such as the fonts, keyboard, and language.*

If XP now starts normally, go to page 41.

If it still doesn't start, reboot into Safe Mode and repeat the above steps, this time with "Load Startup Items." If XP starts after doing this then go to page 41.

If there's still no joy then go to the next page.

# Repairing the XP Installation

The first thing you must do is ensure your system is set to boot from the CD-ROM drive – see page 20.

For this procedure on this page to work, your system must be configured so that the CD-ROM drive is the first boot device. This is done in the BIOS setup program.

Reboot the PC with the XP installation disk in the CD drive. At the bottom of the second boot screen you will see a message saying "Press any key to boot from CD." Do so.

1 At the first screen, select the first option – Set up Windows XP.

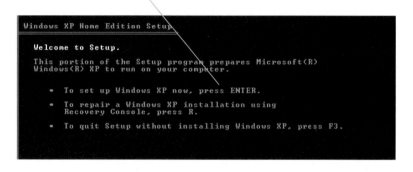

The Repair option will remove any updates you have previously installed that are not included on the XP CD. Drivers will also be reverted to their original XP versions. Some settings such as network and performance settings may be reset to their defaults. However, it won't delete your data, installed programs, personal information or user settings.

Note that the repair procedure will remove any Microsoft Service Packs you have installed. As these contain critical security updates, do not go online before enabling a firewall, particularly if you are using a broadband connection.

2 At the second screen, choose to repair the existing XP installation by pressing R.

The XP installation will now be repaired. However, all your data, applications and settings will remain as they were before.

If there is no operating system listed as shown in step 2 above, then the XP installation is damaged beyond repair. In this situation you will have no alternative but to do a new installation. See pages 56–57 for instructions.

# Selective Startup

*Selective Startup allows you to selectively enable and disable various phases of the startup process. It is useful in determining which phase of the startup process is loading the driver or service causing problems. Selective Startup has its own sub-categories.*

*Process SYSTEM.INI File and WIN.INI File – these options are useful in helping to determine if an older startup application or service is causing problems.*

*Load Startup Services – this option is useful in determining if one of the services that Windows XP loads at startup is causing problems.*

*Load Startup Items – this option is useful in determining if one of the programs Windows starts during the boot process is causing problems.*

You've arrived on this page because deselecting one of the Process SYSTEM.INI file, Process WIN.INI file, or Load Startup Items, in the System Configuration Utility as detailed on page 39, has enabled you to get XP started.

Using the Process SYSTEM.INI file as an example, you now need to establish exactly what entry in that file is causing the problem.

Open the System Configuration Utility by going to Start, Run and typing MSCONFIG in the Run box.

1 Click the SYSTEM.INI tab and then expand the + signs.

## System Configuration Utility

| General | SYSTEM.INI | WIN.INI | BOOT.INI | Services | Startup |

- ☑ ; for 16-bit app support
  - ☐ [drivers]
    - ☐ ;msconfig wave=mmdrv.dll
    - ☐ ;msconfig timer=timer.drv
  - ☐ ;msconfig [mci]
  - ☐ ;msconfig [driver32]
  - ☐ [386enh]
    - ☐ ;msconfig woafont=dosapp.FON
    - ☐ ;msconfig EGA80WOA.FON=EGA80WOA.FON
    - ☐ ;msconfig EGA40WOA.FON=EGA40WOA.FON
    - ☐ ;msconfig CGA80WOA.FON=CGA80WOA.FON
    - ☐ ;msconfig CGA40WOA.FON=CGA40WOA.FON

Move Up · Move Down · Enable · Disable · Find · New · Edit

Enable All · Disable All

OK · Cancel · Apply · Help

*When changes are made with the System Configuration Utility, Windows will notify you of the changes every time you reboot the computer. To prevent this, tick the checkbox at the bottom of the notification dialog box the first time it is displayed.*

3 Enable the first item then click OK.    2 Click Disable All.

Reboot the computer. If XP starts OK then you know the first item is not the cause of the problem. Repeat steps 1 to 3 for all the items, rebooting each time until XP fails to start. The last item enabled will be what's been causing the problem.

Use the above procedure on the Process SYSTEM.INI file, Process WIN.INI file and Load Startup Items.

# Fixing XP with the Recovery Console

*You can run the Recovery Console from the XP CD. However, you can also install it to your drive by doing the following: Place your XP CD in the CD-ROM drive and then go to Start, Run. In the Run box type the following: D:\i386\winnt32.exe /cmdcons where "D" is the letter of your CD drive.*

XP's Recovery Console is a powerful repair utility that enables you to copy, delete, partition and format hard disks, and stop/start services, among other tasks. You can even format the drive XP is installed on, so be careful. It is not an easy tool to get to grips with, however, and demands an understanding of XP's inner workings that the average user just won't have.

For this reason, we won't go into it too deeply. However, we will see how to use it in resolving two very common XP startup issues that have plagued many users.

### C:\windows\system32\config\system File is Missing or Corrupt

The Config\system file is loaded into the system's registry, and if it is corrupted in any way XP simply won't start. It just stops with the above error message. If you ever encounter this, do the following:

*There is a documented bug with the Recovery Console that can affect XP installations preinstalled by manufacturers using a deployment tool called Sysprep. The effect of this bug is that when you type the administrator password, you get a message saying the password is invalid, with the result that the Recovery Console won't start.*

*The solution is to obtain the Q308402 hotfix from Microsoft. Unfortunately, Microsoft have for reasons best known to themselves, seen fit to not make this available for download. Instead, you have to contact them directly and request it.*

1 Reboot with the XP installation CD in the CD-ROM drive.

2 At the Welcome to Setup screen, press R to select "To repair Windows XP installation using Recovery Console."

3 Type the number of the installation that you want to access from the Recovery Console, and press Enter.

4 Type the administrator password when you are prompted to do so, and then press Enter. If no administrator password exists, just press Enter.

5 Type: CD C:\Windows\System32\Config and press Enter.

*When Windows XP is installed, it automatically creates a backup copy of the Config\system file and saves it in the Windows folder. This backup includes the settings for all applications and hardware on the computer at the time of installation. Because step 3 opposite replaces the current (damaged) Config\system file with the backup copy, all applications installed after the XP installation will need to be reinstalled.*

*If you are getting the "NTLDR is Missing" error message while you are attempting to upgrade to Windows XP from Windows 95, Windows 98 or Windows Me, try the following:*

*Boot the computer with a Windows 95, Windows 98 or Windows Me boot floppy disk. Choose option 2 and when you see the A:\> prompt type: SYS C: and press Enter. You should receive the "System Transferred" message. Once this has been completed, remove the floppy disk and reboot the computer.*

6    When you see the prompt again, type: REN system system.old and then press Enter.

7    At the prompt again type: COPY C:\Windows\Repair\system and press Enter.

8    Remove the Windows XP CD and exit the Recovery Console by typing EXIT at the prompt. Restart the computer.

This replaces the corrupted Config folder with a backup copy that was made when XP was run successfully for the first time. Unfortunately, this does mean that all applications and hardware installed since that date will have to be reinstalled. More importantly, however, all your data will still be intact.

### NTLDR is Missing

This error message indicates that XP's boot files are seriously corrupted. Repair as described below:

1    Place the XP installation disk in the CD-ROM drive.

2    Open the Recovery Console at the command prompt.

```
Microsoft Windows XP(TM) Recovery Console.

The Recovery Console provides system repair and recovery functionality.

Type EXIT to quit the Recovery Console and restart the computer.

1: C:\WINDOWS

Which Windows installation would you like to log onto
<To cancel, press ENTER>? 1
Type the Administrator password:
C:\WINDOWS>Copy D:\i386\ntldr c:_
```

3    Type COPY D:\i386\ntldr C: and press Enter. (If your CD-ROM drive is not D:, amend this command as necessary.)

4    Then type COPY ntdetect.com C: and press Enter.

Reboot and XP will now start.

# Creating an XP Disaster Recovery Kit

*Although we use PowerQuest's Drive Image utility to illustrate the procedure in this section, there are many others available on the market. You might even find one or two on the Internet available as a free download.*

If followed correctly, the procedures outlined in this chapter should enable anyone to get XP running, no matter how serious the issue (as long as it is an XP issue and not a hardware one).

The problem is, though, they can take time, a lot of time. This applies particularly if the worst happens and you have to do a complete new installation. This will mean reinstalling all your applications and setting up the PC again just as you want it.

The way round all this is to have a disaster recovery kit, which will enable you to get your system up and running in minutes rather than hours. This will, however, initially require some time and possible expenditure on your part, but it's well worth doing. You will need the following:

*A second hard drive, as long as you are capable of installing and setting it up, is another good backup medium. You also gain extra storage space for other purposes.*

- A disk imaging utility such as PowerQuest's Drive Image.

- A backup medium (recordable CD or a second hard drive).

There are two ways you can go. The first is to simply copy your entire setup to a second hard drive. Drive Image has a drive copy function that will do this. You might, however, need to splash out on a new hard drive. You will also need to know how to install, partition and format it.

The second way is to use recordable CDs. If you don't have a CD writer then get one – they are cheap to buy and simple to install.

*Ideally, when creating your backup, you will do so from a new "clean" installation. By doing this you won't also be backing up any existing problems and niggles. Over time, any Windows installation becomes clogged up with redundant data, cross linked files, invalid shortcuts, etc. This has the effect of noticeably slowing down system performance. It doesn't make much sense to back up a system in this state. A backup of a new installation will allow you to restore your PC to an "as new" state in literally a few minutes.*

The following procedure is, in my opinion, the ideal way to back up your entire system. However, there may be steps that you may wish to skip, depending on your circumstances and needs.

1 Back up your existing data (recordable CD or hard drive).

2 Using the XP installation CD, create and format two partitions on your hard disk (Drive C and Drive E – Drive D is your CD-ROM drive). Drive C is for installing XP, Drive E is for your applications. Assuming you have a 40 GB hard drive, make the first partition about 5 GB and the second 35 GB. See pages 56–57 for how to create and format partitions.

*If you find the idea of partitioning and formatting daunting, then simply skip steps 1 to 4. You will, though, end up with an exact copy of your existing setup, warts and all. Furthermore, you will also be backing up all your applications as well, which could result in a large number of backup CDs.*

*Drive Image will prompt you to create two rescue disks. Do so, as these will enable you to restore XP from DOS – you won't need access to XP.*

*When restoring an image created with Drive Image, you will lose any data created since the backup was made. So remember to back up your data on a regular basis. Include such things as emails, Internet favorites, and personal data. Also, any programs installed after the backup was made will need reinstalling.*

*XP also has a backup utility. However, users of the Home edition will need to manually install it from the XP CD. See page 169.*

3   Install XP to Drive C and then your programs to Drive E.

4   Reinstall your backed-up data, then set up the PC exactly as you want it. Spend some time on this because if you ever have to use the recovery kit, this is the set-up you will get.

5   Now install and run Drive Image.

6   Follow the instructions to create an image of Drive C using your CD-R as the destination. When finished, you will see a summary as shown below.

**Create Image**

Ready to create an image of drive(s) C:, and write data to disk image file F: \MyBackup.pqi

This operation will require about 10 - 19 CD's.

One or more of the operations you have made require rebooting to complete. If you click Yes, the computer will reboot to perform the disk operations.

Perform the operations now?

[ Yes ]   [ No ]   [ Details... ]

7   You will see the approximate number of required CD-Rs.

8   Click Yes.

Drive Image will now reboot the PC and perform the backup. As the CDs are written, you will be requested to place new ones in the CD-ROM drive until the operation is complete. Label them sequentially and put them somewhere safe.

Hopefully, you can see the beauty of this setup. You've only backed up the XP installation itself and your program's configuration files (all on Drive C). The programs themselves, which form the main bulk of your data, are on Drive E. This means your backup should be no more than 2 GB (possibly much less), which Drive Image will fit on to two to three CDs. Thus, should you ever have a problem with XP, you can reinstall it in literally a few minutes. Your programs will still be there on Drive E and will work as normal. Your settings will also be intact.

# XP Shutdown Issues

Many users have reported problems when it comes to shutting down Windows XP. There seem to be three main variations:

### XP Won't Shut Down At All (Stops Responding)

This is the most common issue and very often the cause is a faulty or incorrectly configured device driver. Troubleshoot this as follows:

Go to Start, Control Panel, System, Hardware, Device Manager.

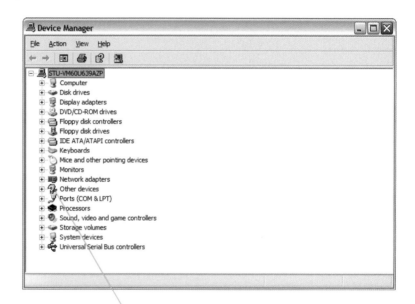

2   Any problem devices will be indicated by a colored symbol.

A yellow exclamation mark means that the device has a problem. A red "X" means that the device is disabled. A blue "i" means that the device has forced resource configurations.

Right-click the entry and click Properties. You will now see a dialog box, which should tell you the nature of the problem. If the message is unspecific, such as "This device has a problem" then reinstalling the device's driver will usually resolve the issue.

Restart the PC and see if XP shuts down now.

The next thing to eliminate is XP's services. To do this you need to open the System Configuration Utility.

1 Go to Start, Run and in the Run box, type MSCONFIG

*XP's services are a class of program that run invisibly in the background, carrying out various functions. However, many of them are often not applicable to a user's operating environment and are thus performing no useful function. As all these services use system resources in terms of CPU and RAM, it makes sense to disable them. Items that can be safely disabled (assuming you aren't networking) are:*

- *Alerter*
- *ClipBook*
- *Fast User Switching*
- *Indexing Service*
- *Net Logon*
- *Network Connections*
- *Print Spooler*
- *Remote Procedure Call*
- *Routing and Remote Access*
- *Secondary Logon*
- *SSDP Discovery Service*
- *Upload Manager*
- *Workstation*

*You can disable them in two ways:*

*1) Click the Services tab in the System Configuration Utility and then deselect them.*

*2) Go to Start, Control Panel, Administrative Services. Click Services. A list of services will now open. Double-clicking each one will give various options such as Starting, Closing and Disabling.*

**System Configuration Utility**

General | SYSTEM.INI | WIN.INI | BOOT.INI | Services | Startup

Startup Selection

○ Normal Startup - load all device drivers and services

○ Diagnostic Startup - load basic devices and services only

◉ Selective Startup

☑ Process SYSTEM.INI File

☑ Process WIN.INI File

☐ Load System Services

☑ Load Startup Items

◉ Use Original BOOT.INI    ○ Use Modified BOOT.INI

[ Launch System Restore ]    [ Expand File... ]

[ OK ]    [ Cancel ]    [ Apply ]    [ Help ]

2 Click Selective Startup and then uncheck the Load System Services box. Click OK.

3 Restart the computer and then try shutting XP down again. If it does shut down then one of the system services is causing the problem. Restart, open the System Configuration Utility again and click the Services tab. Then, one by one, reenable them, rebooting each time until the shutdown problem reappears. The last item enabled will be the source of the problem.

4 If the problem is still present after disabling System Services then repeat the procedure with the Process WIN.INI file, Process System.INI file and Process BOOT.INI file.

If none of this resolves the issue then go on to the next page.

XP can be configured to clear the Page file (see page 99), when the PC is shut down. This is done by changing a registry setting, and many people do it in the belief that it improves system performance. Whether it actually does is a moot point, but what it certainly does do is slow the shutdown procedure considerably. Check this out as follows:

1. Open the registry editor by typing regedit in the Start Menu Run box.
2. Navigate to the following key: HKEY_LOCAL_MACHINE\ System\CurrentControlSet\ Control\Session Manager\ Memory Management
3. Set ClearPageFileAtShutdown value to 0 to disable it or 1 to enable it.

A non-responding service is another cause of slow shutdowns. However, there is a registry setting called WaitToKillServiceTimeout that allows you to specify the length of time that the Service Control Manager must wait for services to complete the shutdown request. Try changing this as follows:

1. Open the registry editor and navigate to HKEY_ LOCAL_MACHINE\System\ CurrentControlSet\Control\ WaitToKillServiceTimeout.
2. Lower the setting and see if the PC shuts down faster now.

If you're still having problems closing XP, disable or uninstall any anti-virus programs you may have running. These applications may still be scanning your drives, thus preventing XP from shutting down.

Next, try disabling these hardware devices in Device Manager: click Sound, video and game controllers; right-click each device in turn and click Disable, rebooting each time. Then do the same for any Network adapters you may have installed.

Reinstall your video driver. If it's a recent addition, try the Driver Rollback option in Device Manager.

As a last resort, restore your system using the System Restore utility. You may well find that this resolves the issue. If you do this, don't forget that any hardware or software installed since the date of the restore point will need reinstalling.

### XP Shuts Down Too Slowly

This problem is caused by a program that has become unstable, so that XP is having trouble closing it down. Usually, a simple reboot will fix the problem. Try rerunning the program and see if it causes the problem again. If it does then reinstall it. Anti-virus software can also cause this problem.

### XP Won't Power Down

When you press the Shutdown button, the PC doesn't actually switch off. You see the "It's Safe to shut down your PC" message.

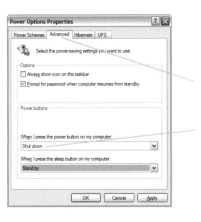

1 Go to Start, Control Panel, Power Options.

2 Click the Advanced tab.

3 In the scrollbox under "When I press the power button on my computer," select Shut down. Then click OK.

# Hard Disk Troubleshooting

## Chapter Five

FACT: One day your hard disk drive will fail. It's as certain as a politician breaking election promises, and you can't get a better guarantee than that!

Disk drives are mechanical devices and as such have a limited life span. When they fail, it's almost always terminal. The average user has no way to repair them.

However, before they fail they usually begin exhibiting signs that indicate they are on the way out. If you wish to avoid losing all your data, you must be able to recognize these signals and act upon them.

It is also a fact that many perceived problems with hard drives are actually nothing of the sort – in reality, they relate to the PC's software environment. These problems can be repaired – if you know how.

This chapter gives you the lowdown on all these issues.

## Covers

# Hard Disk Fault Symptoms

*Is it possible to get a disk drive that's failed working again? Usually, the problem is due to the fact that the drive's mechanics are quite literally stuck.*

*By removing the drive and giving it a sharp tap, it's sometimes possible to get it running again. Not for long, but maybe long enough to copy its data across to a new drive. You've nothing to lose by giving this a try.*

*Another temporary cure, supposedly, is to place the drive in your freezer for a few hours. The theory is that the cold will cause the metal components to contract, thus freeing them up. Try this at your own risk though.*

Because of its importance as a repository for all your data, you might think it would be nice of a hard disk drive to notify you when it's about to fail. You would then have time to safely transfer all your data to a new drive.

Well, actually they do. But are you listening?

Abrupt failure of a disk drive is very rare: usually you will get plenty of warning. The following are all symptoms of a failing drive:

- Unusual amount of disk activity (thrashing).

- Slow spin-up speed.

- Excessive noise (nasty clanking or grinding sounds).

- Chkdsk runs frequently.

- Excessive heat.

- Frequent error messages.

One of the first indications of impending failure is a noticeable increase in the amount of noise your drive is making. This is a sure sign of mechanical wear and tear. The bearings in the drive's motor are usually one of the first of your drive's components to fail – beware, the writing is on the wall.

*If you are unfortunate enough to have a hard drive fail on you that contains data you cannot afford to lose, there are specialist firms who can sometimes retrieve that data for you. This can be extremely expensive, however, and there are no guarantees. You might get all, some, or none of it back.*

This in turn leads to excessive heat being generated, as the motor has to work harder to overcome the frictional drag caused by the sticky bearings. Things are going downhill fast now. If you take the trouble to remove the system case, you'll find the drive is very hot (warm is normal).

One thing leads to another, and soon the drive is taking longer and longer to spin up when you start the PC. Data transfer speeds slow down and general system performance drops off. Chkdsk runs frequently and finds problems each time.

Take note! The drive is warning you that it's soon going to fail completely. If you don't wish to lose all your data, back it up now. Then buy yourself a new model.

# Troubleshooting Hard Disk Failure

*All BIOS setup programs have a facility for password protection.*
*It's quite common for PC manufacturers to enable this and set a password, thus locking you out.*
*If you come up against this problem, try the following:*
*1. Reboot the PC to an A:\> prompt with an old Windows startup disk.*
*2. Type debug then hit Enter.*
*3. At the debug prompt, type o 70 2e and hit Enter again.*
*4. Type 0 71 ff and hit Enter.*
*5. Finally, type q and hit Enter.*
*Reboot the PC, access the BIOS Setup program, and the password prompt should have disappeared.*
*While this works with most BIOS's, we cannot guarantee it will work with all. It's worth a try though.*
*Note that this procedure will reset all the BIOS settings to the factory default settings. Any changes made by the manufacturer and/or user will be lost.*

Major hard drive problems usually manifest themselves when the computer is booted up. The boot procedure stops and you will usually see an error message. Unfortunately, these messages can be on the cryptic side, and will be meaningless to many people – the "NTLDR is missing" message being a typical example.

However, if you can decipher these error messages you are well on the way to isolating the problem.

Usually, if there is a serious problem with your hard drive you will get one of the following errors:

1) Boot-up stops on the first boot screen at the "Detecting IDE Drives" stage. You might get an error message as well.

2) Boot-up stops on the second boot screen with a "Disk Boot Failure" error message.

Either of these indicates one of two things:

- The disk drive is incorrectly configured in the BIOS.

- There is a physical problem with the disk drive.

Error 2 above can also be caused by a missing or severely corrupted operating system (see Startup Troubleshooting).

First, establish if the system has recognized the drive. Reboot, then hold down the BIOS Setup entry key (usually the Delete key). The BIOS Setup program will open. Using the arrow keys, scroll to the CMOS Settings page.

*Different systems will allocate different keys with which to enter the BIOS. These are usually F1, F2, ESC or DEL. In most cases, though, it's the Delete key. There is usually a line of text at the bottom of the boot screen that tells you "Press xxx to Enter Setup."*

```
            Phoenix - AwardBIOS CMOS Setup Utility
                    Standard CMOS Features

Date (mm:dd:yy)          Fri, March 26 2004         Item Help
Time (hh:mm:ss)          14 : 1 : 10

IDE Primary Master       [ST34001400A]              Menu Level
IDE Primary Slave        [None]
IDE Secondary Master     [None]                     Press (Enter)to
IDE Secondary Slave      [None]                     enter next page
                                                    for details of
Drive A                  [1.44M 3.5]                hard drive
Drive B                  [None]

Video                    [EGA\VGA]
Halt On                  [All Errors]

Base Memory              640K
Extended Memory          522346K
Total Memory             522346K
```

Your drive should be listed next to IDE Primary Master.

*The BIOS is contained within a CMOS chip on the mainboard. This chip is powered by an independent battery so that its settings will be retained even in the event of a power failure. This is important, as these settings are crucial to the boot-up procedure.*

*For this reason, be very careful when making changes to any BIOS settings, as it's possible to render the system inoperable.*

*Should you manage to do this, however, you will see a key at the bottom of the main screen (often the F6 key) that will enable you to load a set of fail-safe default settings. This will get the system going again. However, these settings won't be the optimal ones – in other words, your system might not run as well as before.*

If the drive is listed, then you know the system is aware of it. Next, you need to make sure the drive is correctly configured in the BIOS.

On the CMOS Settings page, highlight your drive model and press Enter. The hard disk Auto-detection page will open.

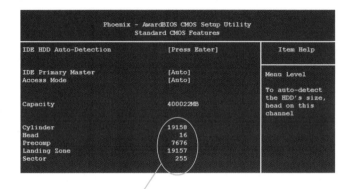

If the drive is correctly configured, its parameters will be listed.

This indicates the disk drive is functioning correctly, and the problem, therefore, is software-related. See Startup Troubleshooting.

If, however, there is no drive listed on the CMOS Settings page (as demonstrated below) then you have a problem with the drive itself, its power supply or its IDE connections.

*If your hard disk is recognized in the BIOS, it's fairly safe to assume that the drive is OK.*

2 No disk drive listed.

Troubleshoot on the next page.

# Is the Drive Unserviceable?

*Before you touch anything inside the system case, ground yourself. Touching anything metal will do. Be particularly careful if you are standing on a carpet. This will generate large amounts of static electricity in your body, which can be a killer for your PC's electronic components.*

The first thing to check is the drive's power supply. Open up the case and unplug the power connector from the drive.

1 You can identify the power connector by its four cables – red, black, black, yellow, in that order.

Now, unplug the power connector from the CD-ROM drive and replace it with the connector that was powering the hard disk drive. Reboot, and if the CD-ROM drive is recognized during the IDE detection stage, then you know it's getting power (and therefore so was the hard disk drive). Switch off, and return the power connectors to their original positions.

*Most hard disk manufacturers have a hard disk diagnostic utility available for download from their websites. Very often you can run the utility directly through your browser.*

The next thing to investigate is the drive's IDE connector, which takes the form of a multicable ribbon.

2 Disk drive IDE Connector.

Make sure the connectors on either end of the cable are firmly seated in their respective sockets – one on the disk drive and the other on the mainboard. If you notice that the ribbon cable is severely twisted or stretched, then there is a slight possibility this is the problem. The individual cables are extremely thin, and it doesn't take much to break them; if there are no physical signs of a problem with the disk drive, check this out by replacing the cable.

*An unusual level of noise coming from the disk drive is a sure sign of impending failure. It might run for several more months without problems, but on the other hand it might not! This is the time to back up your data.*

Finally, if the drive is extremely hot, this is a sure sign of a problem. Get your ear close as you reboot. With a drive that's running normally, you'll be able to hear the platters spin up. If you can't, or they spin up and then back down immediately, this is another indication.

If you want to be 100 percent sure before throwing the drive away, try installing it in another machine.

# Hard Disk Performance Factors

The more your hard disk fills up with data, the worse the effect of fragmentation. To minimize fragmentation as far as possible, always have at least 20 percent of your disk free.

A hard disk is a very dependable device (within its life span) and can usually be relied upon to give a few years of trouble-free operation. However, keeping hard disks running at peak efficiency does require a certain amount of maintenance.

## Hard Disk is Running Slowly

There are various issues that can a cause a disk drive to run below par, all of which are straightforward enough to put right.

A common problem users have when running a disk defragmentation utility is that it keeps restarting – the process never completes.

The reason this happens is that the user is running other applications at the same time. These interfere with the defragmentation procedure thus causing it to keep restarting.

The usual culprits are programs that activate suddenly, such as screensavers, anti-virus software and disk management utilities.

Probably the most common reason is fragmentation. This process is the inevitable result of the constant saving and deleting of data that happens when a computer is used. Over a period of time, individual parts of a file will become separated (fragmented) and thus will be located on different sections of the disk. When a user opens that file, the drive's read/write heads have to hunt about to find all the fragments of the file, which makes retrieval of the file a longer process. A severely fragmented drive will perform much more slowly than it should.

To rectify this situation, XP provides a disk defragmentation utility, which can be found at Start, All Programs, Accessories, System Tools, Disk Defragmenter. Run this application once a week to keep your drive in good order.

Direct Mode Access (DMA) is a method of disk drive data transfer that speeds up a hard drive's performance considerably.

If your system supports DMA, XP should enable it by default. However, it doesn't always do so. See page 68 for details on how to check this out.

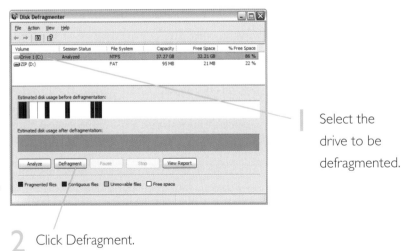

Select the drive to be defragmented.

2   Click Defragment.

*In the early days of computers, viruses were spread mainly by floppy disk. The Internet, however, has provided a much easier way for viruses to be spread. This has reached the point whereby virtually all viruses are now acquired via the Web. Therefore, before running any downloaded application or opening any email, scan them first with a virus checker.*

## Is There a Virus on Your Drive?

Viruses can have all sorts of effects on a computer, including severe degradation of system performance.

If your PC suddenly develops tortoise-like tendencies, particularly after downloading something from the Internet, suspect this immediately. Scan your system with an up-to-date virus program.

## Hard Disk Controller Drivers

The disk controller acts as an interface between the operating system and the drive. As with all hardware devices, it needs a driver to "introduce" it to Windows. It's not unknown for these drivers to become corrupt – when they do, the drive's performance can take a serious hit.

Check this out as follows:

*A hard disk controller consists of a microchip and associated circuitry that is responsible for controlling a disk drive. There are different controllers for different interfaces; for example, an IDE interface requires an IDE controller, and a SCSI interface requires a SCSI controller.*

*With modern hard disk drives, the controller is an integral part of the unit as opposed to being part of the mainboard as they used to be.*

1 Go to Start, Control Panel, System, Hardware, Device Manager. Right-click Primary IDE Channel.

```
Device Manager
File  Action  View  Help

STU-VM60U639AZP
  Computer
  Disk drives
  Display adapters
  DVD/CD-ROM drives
  Floppy disk controllers
  Floppy disk drives
  IDE ATA/ATAPI controllers
    Primary IDE Channel
    Secondary IDE Channel
    VIA Bus Master IDE Controller
  Keyboards
  Mice and other pointing devices
  Monitors
  Network adapters
  Other devices
  Ports (COM & LPT)
  Processors
  Sound, video and game controllers
  Storage volumes
  System devices
```

2 In the right-click menu, click Uninstall.

3 Reboot the PC. On restart XP will automatically reinstall the hard disk's controller driver. To complete the installation, XP will advise you that the system needs to be restarted again; do so.

# Newly Installed Drive Won't Work

Before you can use a new hard disk, you have to partition and format it. With previous versions of Windows, this involved Startup disks and DOS, which many people found somewhat daunting. XP makes the procedure quite straightforward.

If you already have an XP installation that you wish to delete so that you can do a new (clean) installation, press D in Step 2. Then go on to Step 3.

Most modern hard drives come with a feature known as S.M.A.R.T. This is a relatively new hard disk technology, which endeavors to safeguard users against losing data due to disk failure.

S.M.A.R.T. continually monitors what's going on inside the disk drive, and when it sees signs of damage, it flashes an alert to the user, thus giving him or her time to back up their data.

It's quite common for people to go out and buy a new hard drive, install it, and then wonder why it doesn't show up in My Computer. The reason is simple. Before any hard drive can be used, it has to be partitioned and then formatted.

The following shows you exactly how it's done with XP.

1    Set the CD-ROM drive as the first boot device, as described on page 20. Place the XP CD in the CD-ROM drive and boot the PC.

```
Windows XP Home Edition Setup

    Welcome to Setup.

    This portion of the Setup program prepares Microsoft(R)
    Windows(R) XP to run on your computer.

        •  To set up Windows XP now, press ENTER.

        •  To repair a Windows XP installation using
           Recovery Console, press R.

        •  To quit Setup without installing Windows XP, press F3.
```

2    At the Welcome to Setup screen, press Enter.

```
Windows XP Home Edition Setup

    The following list shows the existing partitions and
    unpartitioned space on this computer.

    Use the UP and DOWN ARROW keys to select an item in the list.

        •  To set up Windows XP on the selected item, press ENTER.

        •  To create a partition in the unpartitioned space, press C.

        •  To delete the selected partition, press D.

    4095 MB Disk 0 at Id 0 on bus 0 on atapi [MBR]
         Unpartitioned space                     4095 MB
```

3    At the next screen, press C to create a partition.

4 The next screen allows you to choose the partition size. By default, XP chooses the maximum size.

It's always a good idea to create a separate partition in which to save your data.
If you then ever have to do a clean install of XP, you won't have to worry about backing up the data first.

```
Windows XP Home Edition Setup

You asked Setup to create a new partition on
4095 MB Disk 0 at Id 0 on bus 0 on atapi [MBR].

   • To create the new partition, enter a size below and
     press ENTER.

   • To go back to the previous screen without creating
     the partition, press ESC.

The minimum size for the new partition is        8 megabytes (MB).
The maximum size for the new partition is     4087 megabytes (MB).
Create partition of size (in MB):  4087
```

5 At the 4th screen, press Enter to Setup XP on the selected item.

The Format screen offers you several options. Which one you choose depends on various factors.
For example, if the installation will form part of a dual/multi boot setup and one of the operating systems is Windows 95, 98 or Me, choosing the FAT option will enable these systems to see your XP installation. If you choose NTFS, they won't.
The Quick format option will not scan the drive for bad sectors, whereas the Full Format will. Only use the Quick option if you are sure the drive is free of errors; if it isn't, you could encounter problems when installing XP.
In general, the best advice is to format with NTFS. This file system is more stable than FAT and will give better performance.

```
Windows XP Home Edition Setup

The following list shows the existing partitions and
unpartitioned space on this computer.

Use the UP and DOWN ARROW keys to select an item in the list.

   • To set up Windows XP on the selected item, press ENTER.

   • To create a partition in the unpartitioned space, press C.

   • To delete the selected partition, press D.

4095 MB Disk 0 at Id 0 on bus 0 on atapi [MBR]

   C: Partition1 [New (Raw)]               4087 MB ( 4086 MB free)
      Unpartitioned space                     8 MB
```

6 Finally, you will see the Format screen. Make your choice and then press Enter.

```
Windows XP Home Edition Setup

The partition you selected is not formatted. Setup will now
format the partition.

Use the UP and DOWN ARROW keys to select the file system
you want, and then press ENTER.

If you want to select a different partition for Windows XP,
press ESC.

   Format the partition using the NTFS file system (Quick)
   Format the partition using the FAT file system (Quick)
   Format the partition using the NTFS file system
   Format the partition using the FAT file system
```

XP will now format the new partition. When this is complete, Setup will begin automatically. The whole procedure is quite straightforward.

NOTE: If you don't wish to install XP on the new drive, but would rather just use it for storage, then just quit Setup as soon as the format procedure has finished.

# Disk Capacity Not Recognized by XP

There is another issue regarding reported disk space. This affects all PCs, regardless of the operating system used. No disk drive will actually have the manufacturer's stated capacity. For example a 120 GB drive will, in reality, have about 112 GB storage capacity. This is due to the capacity measurement units used by the manufacturers. This is too complex an issue to explain here, but be assured it's not a fault with your disk drive or PC; it affects us all.

Be very wary of using Dynamic Drive Overlay on a dual/multi boot system. This type of setup uses a boot manager, which allows you to choose the operating system to boot up. Unfortunately, Dynamic Drive Overlay doesn't work reliably with boot managers and can cause major problems – even the complete loss of all data on a drive.

Also, use of disk management utilities such as Partition Magic can have similarly drastic consequences when used with Dynamic Drive Overlay.

You've gone out and bought a nice new 60 GB hard disk, correctly installed, partitioned and formatted it, only to find XP is reporting it as having a size of 32 GB.

This is not a fault as such. You've done nothing wrong, the drive is OK and XP is reading it correctly. The problem is due to the system's BIOS.

Unfortunately, many, if not most, BIOS programs come with a limitation that prevents them recognizing more than 32 GB of a hard drive's capacity.

There are two methods of getting round this problem:

- Update the BIOS.

- Install a disk manager.

The first method we have already covered (see page 33). However, this is not guaranteed to do the trick, as it would appear that the writers of some BIOS programs are lagging behind the times. Even with the latest BIOS updates, many users are finding the problem still exists.

The second method is the most simple and does work. Fortunately, hard disk manufacturers are aware of the BIOS limitation issue and they all have available a disk manager utility, which resolves the problem by installing a Dynamic Drive Overlay. This overrides the BIOS and effectively tricks it into seeing the drive's full capacity.

If your hard drive came with an installation CD, you should find the utility there. If not, you can download it from the relevant manufacturer's website.

These utilities also come with partitioning, formatting and drive copying facilities, and are actually well worth having even if you don't use the Dynamic Drive Overlay facility.

# CD/DVD/Floppy Drive Troubleshooting

Although CD-ROM/DVD-ROM and floppy drive units employ totally different technologies, for troubleshooting purposes they are very similar, and thus will be considered the same unless otherwise stated.

Faults with the actual drive mechanisms are rare, and are usually restricted to issues with accumulated dust and grime.

Most problems that occur relate to the media used by the device. This is because removable media is extremely susceptible to physical damage, and many problems result from careless media storage and handling.

## Covers

**Chapter Six**

# Drive Doesn't Work

Faults with drive unit mechanisms are rare. Most problems are a result of damaged media. Accumulated grime in the drive's inner workings can also cause problems.

You've put a disc in the drive and tried to play it, but it refuses to start. AutoPlay doesn't work, and the drive's icon might or might not be present in My Computer.

The first thing to establish is whether the drive is being recognized by Windows. Do this as follows:

> Go to Start, Control Panel, System, Hardware, Device Manager. If your drive is being recognized by the system, it will be listed in the DVD/CD-ROM or Floppy disk category in Device Manager.

If your drive unit is defective, given the low prices of these devices nowadays (floppy drives in particular) it's hardly worth the bother of trying to repair it; simply replace it with a new model.

Having said this, if the unit in question is one of the newer multi format DVD drives (which are not so cheap) it might be worth attempting a repair.

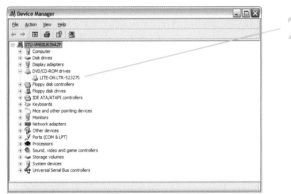

2 Right-click the device, click Properties and make sure it hasn't been disabled in the Device Usage box.

If it isn't listed at all then the device's driver hasn't been installed or is corrupt. Reinstall it by using the Add Hardware wizard in the Control Panel. If the device came with an installation CD or floppy disk, have this to hand.

If there is still no joy then you have a problem with the device itself or its connections. The first thing to check is that it is getting power. If the LED (light) works, or you can hear physical activity, then power is present. If not, check as described on page 26.

A simple way of checking the drive's power supply is to temporarily connect the power cable to a different drive in the PC. If the other drive works then you know the power supply is OK.

If the device was working and then suddenly stopped, it is unlikely that there will be a problem with the connections unless something has happened that could have dislodged them. Open the system case and make sure all plugs are seated firmly in their sockets.

The only other explanation is a defective drive unit. Replace it.

# Media Issues

*Disc media are susceptible to physical damage. Handle and store them with care to avoid scratching them.*

*Prolonged exposure to strong sunlight will render disc media useless.*

*If you have a badly damaged disc that contains data you can't afford to lose, try a CD data recovery utility. These programs can be downloaded from the Internet and will recover data from severely scratched or otherwise damaged discs, although the recovery procedure can take a very long time.*

*If your CD tray is stuck, preventing you from removing a CD, switch off, restart and try again. If that doesn't work, push a small pin or straightened-out paper clip into the tiny hole at the front of the CD drive. This will force the drive to open the tray.*

## Discs Don't Play Properly

Some files on a disc won't open (while others will), you receive file copy error messages or the disc won't run at all: These problems are all indicative of a damaged or dirty disc, which is likely to have been caused through careless handling.

Inspection of the disc will reveal scratches and/or foreign matter contaminating the surface of the disc. Clean the disc with a soft lint-free material and then try it again.

If the disc is scratched, it is sometimes possible to restore it to working condition (depending on the severity of the damage). A CD/DVD disc is comprised of various layers of material, the outermost layer being a thin protective film of aluminum. Because the data track is below this layer, it is sometimes possible to remove the scratches without damaging the data.

For this you will need a very fine household abrasive, such as brass or silver polish. Using a clean cloth gently rub the surface of the disc until the scratches have been removed as far as possible.

## Discs Open Slowly or Freeze the Computer

If you find that the drive appears to be working intermittently – some discs won't play at all while others take ages to load up – the problem will almost certainly be a dirty laser lens or mirror inside the drive unit. If this is the case, you will also quite probably be experiencing crashes and lock-ups when loading discs.

The solution, not surprisingly, is to clean the drive's lens. This is not a particularly difficult thing to do, but many people will probably be tempted to try one of the proprietary lens cleaning discs available on the market. Unfortunately, they will almost certainly be wasting their time and money. These discs are next to useless as all they actually do is remove any loose dust, which is not likely to be causing the problem anyway.

If you're not prepared to, or capable of, opening up the drive unit and cleaning the lens/mirror properly, then your only option is to throw it away and buy a new one.

# DVD-Specific Issues

*Not all systems can handle the heavy demands made of them by DVD video. If you have added a DVD drive to an existing system (rather than purchasing a system containing a DVD drive) it's possible that your system simply isn't up to the job. If this is the case you might well need to upgrade your CPU, RAM and possibly also your video adapter.*

*If you intend to use DVDs a lot, it would make sense to invest in a video adapter that has a DVD decoder built in (i.e. a hardware decoder).*

*It will also help to make sure that the latest version of DirectX is installed. This can be obtained from the cover CDs of PC magazines or downloaded from the Microsoft website.*

### DVDs Won't Play At All

The first thing to check is that you have a DVD decoder installed. XP doesn't have native support for DVD file formats, and so a third-party decoder must be installed to decode the DVD signals into a format that XP will recognize.

If this is the case, you should get an error message telling you that a decoder needs to be installed. If you have been able to play DVDs before then try rebooting the PC; this might do the trick.

If the DVD still won't play and you have a decoder installed then reinstall it. If it's a hardware decoder, you might also need to update the decoder's firmware, which should be available from the manufacturer's website.

You could also try playing the DVD with different playback software, such as Windows Media Player.

### DVD Playback is Broken Up

Restart the computer. This will ensure the PC is running in a stable condition, which can make the difference between acceptable and unacceptable playback.

Enabling Direct Mode Transfer (DMA) on systems that support it can improve performance. Check this out as described on page 68.

DVD playing is very demanding of system resources, and if yours aren't up to the job then poor performance can result. Make sure no other applications are running – in particular programs that make use of video overlay techniques, such as video capture applications.

*Before spending money on upgrading your system, try obtaining and installing any available updates for your existing decoder and video adapter. Doing this will often be enough to improve performance to an acceptable level.*

You can also try lowering color depth and screen resolution as described on pages 82 and 83. Your decoder might not have enough memory to support the color depth and screen resolution currently selected.

If the problem persists, try updating your video adapter driver. Also, install any updates available for the decoder.

Don't forget the DVD disc itself. Just as with CDs, any dirt or scratches on the surface of the disc can result in jerky and intermittent performance.

# DVD's & Regional Coding

*Another issue that might prevent a DVD from playing is that of the manufacturer's copy protection.*

*Unlike home DVD drives, PC DVD drives allow users to copy movies and games. Often these are given to friends and family. As with regional coding, many manufacturers are introducing some form of copy protection to try and prevent this.*

*Some manufacturers are now using copy protection techniques that are so strict that people are finding that discs they have purchased quite legitimately, are refusing to play. While one can sympathize with the film companies to an extent, this simply is not acceptable. The solution in this situation must be to buy elsewhere.*

*There are now many specialist electronic companies offering modifications to remove the region code lock-outs from DVD players.*

You try and play a DVD, but get a message saying you cannot play the DVD in this region (or words to that effect).

This problem is due to the paranoia of the movie studios. In an effort to limit the loss of revenue caused by illegal copying, they have introduced a system of regional coding whereby DVDs marketed in one part of the world cannot be played in another.

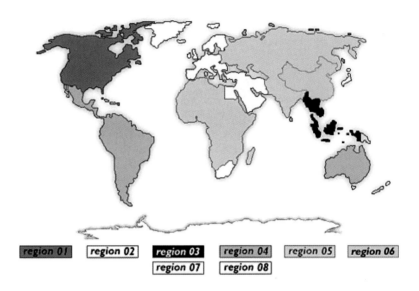

region 01 | region 02 | region 03 | region 04 | region 05 | region 06
region 07 | region 08

The world shown split into six DVD regions. 7 & 8 are not assigned.

If you live in the USA, and try playing a DVD marketed in Europe, you will get a regional error message. So, if this is your situation, is there anything you can do to get your DVD playing?

The answer is yes. Quite legally, you can change the regional code of your DVD drive a limited number of times (usually 5) to match that of the DVD.

Before you can do this though, you need to know the regional code of the DVD you are trying to play. This is simple, as it is usually displayed on the DVD box as a number on a world globe. Once you know this you can set your DVD player to match as described overleaf:

*The unpopularity of region coding has created a market for so-called Code Free DVD players, which are essentially modified versions of standard DVD players in which the region coding function has been disabled. While not strictly legal, these are, nevertheless, widely available. Owners of these players can purchase and play DVDs from any region. As a countermeasure, the movie companies are retaliating with Regional Coding Enhancement.*

1 Go to Start, Control Panel, System, Hardware & Device Manager.

2 Right-click your DVD drive and then click Properties.

3 Click the DVD Region tab.

4 Click the geographic area that corresponds with the DVD and then click OK.

NOTE: You can change the region code of your DVD drive a limited number of times. If "Changes Remaining" reads 1 and you select a new region, you will never be able to play DVDs from any other region on that drive.

You may also run into problems if you are using one of the multi-region players now available on the market, or one that has been "doctored" to be region-free. You will see the following message:

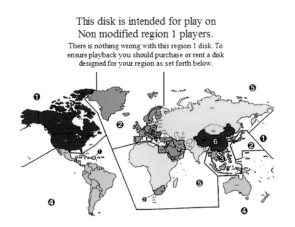

This disk is intended for play on Non modified region 1 players.
There is nothing wrong with this region 1 disk. To ensure playback you should purchase or rent a disk designed for your region as set forth below.

If you see this message it means that the DVD has an additional layer of protection, known as Regional Coding Enhancement.

Regional Coding Enhancement is a form of digital protection, which some manufacturers have placed on selected Region 1 DVDs to prevent them from playing on region-free or multi-region players.

# Autoplay Doesn't Work

Autoplay is a Windows feature that automatically opens a relevant program when a CD, DVD or Zip disk is inserted. If you find that certain types of disk (for example video disks) aren't opening automatically, check it out as follows:

*Should you wish to do so, it is possible to disable XP's Autoplay on a disc-by-disc basis simply by pressing the shift key on the keyboard as the disc is inserted.*

1 Click My Computer and then right-click your CD/DVD/Zip drive.

2 Click Properties and then click the Autoplay tab.

3 Select the type of disc that won't autoplay, e.g. video.

4 Make sure that the Take no action option has not been selected.

If Autoplay doesn't work at all, check it isn't disabled in the registry:

1 Click Start, Run. In the Run box type REGEDIT. Click OK.

2 In the Registry Editor, locate the following registry key: HKEY_CURRENT_USER\Software\Microsoft\Windows\CurrentVersion\Policies\Explorer\NoDriveTypeAutoRun

*An example of a CD-burning application that can prevent Autoplay from working is any version of Roxio's Easy CD Creator that is earlier than version 5.02d. If you have any of these installed on your system, an upgrade is available from Roxio's website. Alternatively, uninstall it.*

3 Double-click NoDriveTypeAutoRun on the right-hand side and make sure that 91 is entered in the Value data box.

If Autoplay has been disabled there is a good chance that a CD-burning application is responsible. Some of these programs will automatically disable Autoplay, as it can interfere with the burning process. If so, either upgrade the program or uninstall it.

# Floppy Disk Issues

Floppy disks are simplicity itself to use, and also have the added benefit of being relatively robust in construction – unlike CDs.

There are only two problems an inexperienced computer user might experience with this type of disk.

## Unformatted Disk

If you find you cannot save a file to a particular floppy disk, it could be that the disk hasn't been formatted. This will only happen with an old disk (modern ones come preformatted). If this is the case you will get an error message to this effect. Format the disk as follows:

*Before any magnetic storage medium can be used, it must be formatted. This procedure organizes the surface of the disk into neat sectors and tracks. These act as signposts to the read/write heads, telling them exactly where to go during file transfer operations.*

1  Open My Computer and right-click the floppy drive icon.

2  From the right-click menu select Format.

*By default, XP does a full format of a floppy disk. This involves not just the formatting procedure, but also a full scan for bad sectors (which can cause subsequent storage and file retrieval problems). The Quick format option just formats the disk – the bad sector scan is not carried out.*

3  Select Quick Format.

4  Click Start.

## Floppy Disk Write-Protection

When a floppy disk is write-protected you will be unable to add to, move or delete its contents. If you try to do any of these, you will get an error message as shown below:

*Write-protection provides a means of ensuring that data cannot be accidently altered or deleted from a floppy disk.*

The solution is to remove the write-protection by sliding the small tab at the back of the disk.

# CD/DVD Burning Troubleshooting

There are very few computers sold these days that don't come with a CD writer or rewriter.

Although disc burning is nothing new, advances in associated technology have, to a certain degree, eliminated the problems that made burning such a hit-and-miss affair in the not so distant past.

Reliable as modern day burners may be, however, there are still other factors involved, which need to be addressed before a disc can be successfully burned.

## Covers

**Chapter Seven**

# Disc Burning Problems

Many of the problems experienced in the early days of CD burning have largely been eliminated by the modern breed of CD burners and mastering programs. However, issues still remain, many of which are a result of users' lack of understanding of the subject rather than faults with the burning process itself. This section highlights the more common of these issues, together with a brief explanation of each.

There are two types of disc: writable and rewritable. The first, CD-R, can be used only once. Once the disc is full you can do no more with it. These discs are the cheapest, quickest to write to, and are the best for data backup. They have a projected useful life of approximately fifty years.

The second type, CD-RW, uses a disc that can be reused several hundred times. These discs are more expensive, and are not recommended for storage of important data due to limitations caused by their composition. They have a projected shelf life roughly half that of a CD-R disc. Recording to them takes considerably longer than to CD-R.

## Disc Fails to Burn

For a disc to be burned successfully, the flow of data from the source must be continuous and at a constant speed – otherwise the burn will fail and usually the disc will be ruined. Anything that interrupts the data flow during the burn process can potentially cause burn errors. Therefore, you need to track down and close anything on your PC that may be doing this.

The following are the usual suspects:

## DMA Enabled

DMA enables devices to communicate without CPU intervention. In most situations this is beneficial. However, it can cause problems in a disc-burning environment. Check if this is the cause of your burns failing by doing the following:

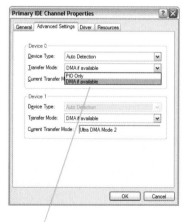

1 Go to Start, Control Panel, System, Hardware, Device Manager.

2 Click IDE ATA/ATAPI IDE Controllers. Right-click the controller for your drive.

3 Click Properties, Advanced Settings.

SmartBurn is a technology developed to prevent disc write errors. It works by "remembering" the exact point at which the burn stops and then resuming at that point when data flow resumes.

4 In the next dialog box, deselect DMA if available.

*Packet writing is a relatively new technique that effectively allows a disc to be used as you would any other fixed drive. For example, you can drag and drop files to the disc, or save to it from an application's "Save" or "Save As" menu command.*

*Packet writing is a very easy way of burning, once you've got to grips with it, but initially it can cause a lot of confusion.*

*Before you can use this method, the disc has to be formatted – this formatting procedure can reduce the disc's available capacity by anything up to 20 percent.*

*Image burning has two slight disadvantages. Firstly, the whole procedure will take twice as long, because the image file has to be created first. Secondly, the image file will need anything up to 800 MB of disk space. This file, however, can be deleted once the burn is complete.*

*Before assuming a burn has failed, consider the possibility that it has in fact succeeded, and that your problem is actually a reading error. See pages 71–72.*

## XP's AutoPlay Function

A few seconds into the burn process, XP will suddenly "see" the new disc and try to read it. This will send an "interrupt" to the CPU, which can cause the burn to fail. For this reason many disc mastering programs will automatically disable AutoPlay. Some don't, however, so check it has been disabled on your system as described on page 65.

## Background Activity

Disable all programs that run invisibly in the background and can suddenly activate, such as screensavers, anti-virus software, disk management utilities and Advanced Power Management.

## Open Applications

Close all other programs that are running. These will be indicated on the Taskbar or in the Task Manager. If the burns still fail, ensure you're not doing any of the following:

## Track At Once (TAO) Burning

The mastering software gives you two ways to burn data:

Track At Once – burning directly from the source to the disc. This is the fastest method, but also the most likely to result in a failed burn (as there is no opportunity to check for errors).

Image Burning – with this method the data is saved to the hard disk as an image file. This process allows potential problems to be identified. The image file is then burned to the disc. If your burns fail with Track At Once, try Image Burning.

1 | Project being saved as a disc image file.

2 | When the file has been created, it is burned to the disc.

## Dual/Multi-Booting

The likelihood of getting burning errors is increased if your mastering software is installed on a system that is part of a dual/multi-boot setup. Try burning on a single system setup.

## Multiple Versions of CD Mastering Software

Having two or more mastering programs installed is not good. These programs often use the same system files and resources and so can prevent each other from working. If this is the case, choose the one you want to use and uninstall the others.

*Windows XP does not get on with some third-party burning software.*

## Burn Speed

Burning at too high a speed can cause errors. This applies particularly to systems with low CPU speed and RAM, which are just not fast enough to keep up. All mastering software has an option that will allow a slower burn speed to be selected.

*If you're consistently getting errors when burning, try lowering the burn speed. Many burning programs will automatically use the highest speed available.*

**Record Setup**

Destination
F:\LITE-ON LTR-52327S

Number of Copies:
1

Write Speed
SmartBurn
12x (1800KB/sec)
16x (2400KB/sec)
24x MAX
32x MAX

Copy to Hard Disk First

☑ Buffer Underrun Prevention

...tion will allow the recorder to automatically record at the optimal speed for the media being used. It is recommended that this option always be used to assure

roxio     OK     Cancel     Help     Details >>

Burn speed options in Roxio's Easy CD Creator.

*Home/car CD players can read music discs only if they have been recorded in the CD Audio Track file format. When you select a mastering software's "Audio Disc" option, any music files are automatically converted to this format before being burned.*

## Unable To Add More Files To a Music Disk

You want to add some music files to a music disc you created earlier, as you can when burning data. However, the mastering program won't let you – it just says "The disc inserted is not blank."

This is not actually a fault, it's done by design. The reason is that you can add files to only a multi-session (open) disc, which is what mastering software will create by default when you burn general data. However, home/car CD players can't read multi-session discs, so the software will create a single-session (closed) disc when you burn music files. Because the disc has been closed, however, you cannot add more files to it later.

# Disc Reading Problems

Assuming a disc has been written successfully and it is clean and free of scratches, you should be able to read or play it. Perceived problems are all too often due to users' lack of knowledge.

## Disc Appears to be Blank

You've opened a disc and there appears to be nothing on it, yet you know it was burned successfully. When you look at the disc's Properties in My Computer you see the following:

*Packet-written discs are not a reliable method of data storage. If you are planning on making a backup of important data, use the mastering program's "Data Disk" option. Also, make sure you use a CD-R disc rather than a CD-RW disc; these are more reliable and have a longer shelf life.*

*Packet writing is best used when you are burning many small files to disc over a period of time – just as you would use a floppy disk in fact.*

*If you want to be able to read UDF formatted discs without installing packet writing software, you can download free UDF readers from the Internet. Roxio offers a "UDF Volume Reader" utility for both the Macintosh and PC.*

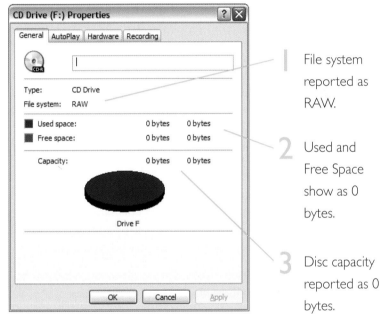

1  File system reported as RAW.

2  Used and Free Space show as 0 bytes.

3  Disc capacity reported as 0 bytes.

This situation occurs when a disc is burned with the UDF file format used by packet writing software. As we explained on page 69, this is a technique that allows the disc to be used as a fixed drive; you can drag and drop files to it just as you would with a floppy disk.

The problem arises when the disk is played on a system that doesn't have packet writing software installed on it. As Windows XP doesn't natively support the UDF file format, the disc will appear to be blank.

To be able to read the disc, you need to install a packet writing application, such as Nero's InCD.

## Disc Closing

A disc burn procedure consists of three stages:

Firstly, the lead-in area is created. This is an area at the start of each session that is left blank for the TOC (table of contents).

Secondly, the data files are written.

*Before a disc can be read, it must be finalized (or closed). This procedure writes out the table of contents (TOC), without which the disc is useless. The exception to this is when a multi-session disc is created.*

*The principal purpose of multiple sessions is to allow additional data to be appended to a previously recorded disc. A session is defined as a data section including lead-in, program data and lead-out.*

*In a multi-session disc, the different sessions are linked together, so that all the disc's data can be read, regardless of which session it was created in. The benefit of multi-session disc burning is that you can fully use the total available space on the disc over a period of time.*

Thirdly, the lead-out area is created. This procedure writes out the table of contents in the lead-in area created at the beginning of the burn, and then closes the disc. If this final step is missed out or not completed then the disc will be unreadable. Multi-session discs are an exception to this: see the margin tip.

A frequent cause of this problem is the user deciding to manually eject the disc before it has been properly closed. Or, the computer may have frozen or crashed as the lead-out was being written. Whichever, this situation is irretrievable – if it's a CD-R, throw it away; if it's a CD-RW, you can reformat it and use it again.

## Music Discs Won't Play On Home/Car CD Player

Home entertainment systems will recognize music files recorded in only the CDFS format. If music files are burned using the mastering software's "Audio Disc" wizard, the files are automatically converted to this format.

However, if they are burned with the packet writing method, they will be in their original format: MP3, WAV, etc. Your PC's CD player will recognize them, but a home player won't.

| Open the disc in My Computer.

2 If the file type is anything other than CD Audio Track, then the files have been recorded in the wrong format, as shown here.

# Miscellaneous Burning/Reading Issues

### Disc Space Reported Incorrectly

Windows reports your 700 MB disc as having approximately 550 MB of free space.

*Reading errors are more likely with CD-RW discs. This applies particularly if you are playing them on an older CD player. Modern players are less likely to have problems.*

*XP's integrated disc burner has one big advantage over third-party packet writing software: while it works just like a packet writer, it does not require the disc to be formatted. Therefore, all the disc's capacity will be available for data storage.*

*If you decide to label your discs with proprietary CD labels, make sure you get them centered as accurately as possible. It doesn't take much to throw a disc off balance.*

**CD Drive (F:) Properties**

General | AutoPlay | Hardware | DLA | Sharing | Recording

Type:     CD Drive
File system:   RAW

Used space:     1,810,432 bytes    1.72 MB
Free space:     565,075,968 bytes   538 MB

Capacity:     566,886,400 bytes   540 MB

Drive F

OK    Cancel    Apply

**1** Free space reported as 538 MB.

**2** This isn't a fault, but rather is due to the disc having being formatted by packet writing software; this typically uses some 150 MB of disc space.

### Burned Games Discs Won't Play

You've borrowed a friend's game and copied it to a disc. Unfortunately, it won't play – you get a "Please Insert Disk" message.

The cause of this is the game manufacturer not wanting you to copy the game – they'd rather you went out and bought it (as you should). In an effort to reduce illegal copying, they copy protect the game so that it will play from only the original disc.

There is nothing you can do about this other than to buy your own copy.

### File Attributes Are Locked

You've tried to change the attributes of a file on a disc, perhaps to compress or hide it. You get an error message though, saying "Access is Denied." This will happen if the disc in question is a CD-R, as you can write to a CD-R only once.

The solution is to copy the file to the hard disk, change the attribute, and then burn it to disk again. You can, however, change file attributes on a CD-RW.

# XP-Specific Issues

XP's burning utility is, on the face of it, a packet writer. You can drag and drop files just as with other packet writing software. However, it is not a packet writer and should not be confused as such.

XP's burner is a very basic example of its type. It doesn't have a user interface, and so it is not possible to select various options and change settings as you can with more advanced burners.

It is not possible to delete individual files from a rewritable disc burned with XP. This is a limitation of the utility. Instead, you have to erase all the disc's contents.

There are several known bugs with XP's disc burner. Visit Microsoft's website for more details and fixes.

Windows XP comes with its own disc mastering facility. All you have to do is drag your files to the drive, as you would with a floppy or hard disk, click "Write these files to CD" and XP will burn them to the disc.

You can access XP's burner settings as follows:

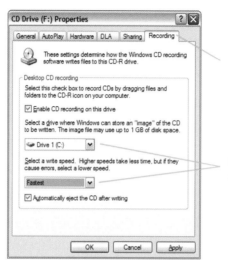

1 Click Start, My Computer. Right click the CD-drive icon and select Properties. Click the Recording tab.

2 Available burning options.

XP's burner is very straightforward – when it works. Unfortunately, there are known issues with it, particularly when third-party mastering software is also installed. These include:

## Disc is Unreadable
You have any of the following symptoms:

- The disc recording is consistently unsuccessful.

- You can't read the disc in any Windows version other than XP.

- You can read the disc in XP but not in an MP3 player.

These problems can be caused by a known bug in XP. The answer is to download the Q320174 package from the Microsoft website.

### Third-Party Software

While some people will be quite content with XP's functional but somewhat limited mastering utility, many will prefer the many features and options offered by programs such as Ahead's Nero and Roxio's Easy CD Creator.

However, some third-party mastering software does not integrate well with XP and can cause the following problems:

*There are other issues that can cause the errors detailed on this page. If you are experiencing any of these and you don't have third-party mastering programs installed, have a look on the Microsoft website, where there are several articles offering causes and solutions.*

*You can also find answers in the many Internet forums available on the subject of disc burning.*

- "Drive is not Accessible" error message.

- The CD/DVD drive is missing from My Computer.

- The Recording tab is missing from the drive's Properties.

- The drive is not recognized as a recordable device.

*As with mastering software, some disc burners do not work well with XP. If you are experiencing problems with yours, make sure the burner's firmware is up-to-date.*

*Firmware is a chip inside the drive unit that acts as its "brain." Firmware upgrades reprogram the chip with the latest technological advances.*

If you experience any of these problems, uninstall all third-party mastering software. If you can identify a particular program as causing problems, go to the manufacturer's website for any available patches.

While on the subject of upgrading, it is also a good idea to upgrade the firmware of your CD/DVD drive, particularly if it is an older model. Firmware upgrades are available for download from the relevant manufacturer's website.

## Disc Burn Does Not Complete Successfully

You get a "Can not complete the CD writing wizard" error message. This may occur if XP's IMAPI CD Burner service is turned off or disabled.

Resolve this issue as follows:

*IMAPI stands for Image Mastering Applications Programming Interface. This service manages XP's CD recording utility. If the service is stopped, the computer will be unable to record CDs, and any services that explicitly depend on it will fail to start.*

*The service is set to Manual by default. However, if you are having problems burning discs, try setting it to Automatic.*

1. Go to Start, Control Panel, Administrative Tools, Services.

2. Locate the IMAPI CD Burning service.

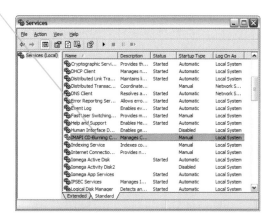

*Certain third-party disc mastering applications can stop or disable the IMAPI service. If you are having burning problems, check this out as described opposite.*

3. Right-click, and select Properties.

4. Make sure the service is not set to Disabled.

5. Make sure the service is not set to Stopped.

# Video/Sound Troubleshooting

Video problems are usually caused by issues relating to the monitor or the PC's video system and/or their settings. These faults are usually fairly simple to isolate and rectify. This chapter explains the more common issues users are likely to experience.

Sound problems are also not too difficult to diagnose and repair, and, more often than not, a reinstallation of the sound card driver is all that's required.

## Covers

Chapter Eight

# No Display (Monitor is Blank)

*A display that is completely blank is probably the most alarming thing to see on a computer. With no information on the screen, you have absolutely no clues as to what could be causing the problem.*

*However, whatever it is, it's unlikely to have just happened out of the blue. These types of fault are usually caused by the user doing something they shouldn't have.*

*If you find yourself in this situation, think back to what you were doing prior to the fault manifesting itself, which might well give you a starting point.*

There are three situations in which you may encounter a display that is completely blank:

- When you boot the computer.

- When XP begins to load.

- When XP is running.

The first scenario (when the PC boots) indicates a hardware problem. Refer to Chapter 3 for details on how to troubleshoot.

If the display goes blank at the point where XP begins to load, you have one of two problems:

- The video adapter driver is missing or corrupt.

- The video adapter's BIOS settings are incorrect.

Reinstall the video adapter driver as follows:

1 Reboot the computer into Safe Mode.

2 When you are back in Windows, go to Start, Control Panel, Hardware, Device Manager. Right-click your video driver (in the Display adapter Category) and click Uninstall.

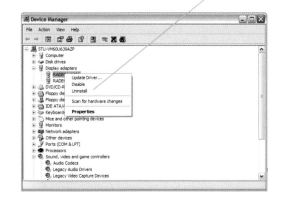

*Another method of installing or reinstalling a video driver is to right-click the Desktop, click Properties, click the Settings tab and then click the Advanced button. Click the Adapter tab and then the Properties button. In the Driver Properties dialog box, click the Driver tab. Here you'll see various options including Uninstall and Update Driver. Clicking the Update Driver button will open the Add New Hardware wizard.*

Reboot the PC in Normal mode, and on restart XP will reinstall the video driver.

When an Advanced Graphics Port (AGP) video adapter is installed, very often AGP will need to be enabled in the system's BIOS. This procedure is described in detail on page 80. You may also need to experiment with some of the settings on a trial and error basis, to get the adapter working optimally.

Selecting the BIOS fail-safe defaults replaces the current BIOS settings with predefined settings that are intended to put the system into as stable a state as possible. In most cases this means the slowest memory timings, performance enhancing features turned off, etc. You can use this option if your system becomes faulty after you make changes in the BIOS in order to return it to a working condition.

Before you make any changes to the BIOS, go through it methodically and make a note of all the settings. Then load the fail-safe defaults as described on this page.

Reboot, and if the video is now working, restore the original BIOS settings one by one, rebooting after each change, until you have located the source of the problem.

You need to do the next step only if you have recently either:

- Changed the BIOS settings.

- Installed a new AGP video adapter.

Resolve the former as follows:

1 Enter the BIOS setup program, as described on page 51.

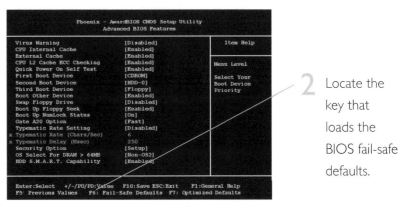

2 Locate the key that loads the BIOS fail-safe defaults.

3 Hit the key (usually the F6 key), save the changes and exit BIOS.

4 Reboot the computer, and the display should now be restored.

This procedure loads a conservative set of BIOS settings, which is pretty much guaranteed to work with any setup.

Note that doing this will also undo any performance enhancing changes that might have previously been made to the BIOS. These will usually have been done by the computer's manufacturer and possibly also the user. You will have to go back to the BIOS and redo these changes – see the margin note.

Don't let this put you off, however. You should find details in your computer manual. Alternatively, there are any number of websites offering full instructions on how to optimally set up a BIOS.

If the fault has occurred after installing a new AGP video adapter, do the following:

*AGP is designed specifically for the demands of 3D video. Rather than using the PCI bus, AGP provides a dedicated channel so that the video controller can directly access the system's memory. The advantage of this is speed.*

*AGP also allows 3D textures to be stored in main memory (RAM) rather than video memory.*

1 Reboot into the BIOS setup program – see page 51.

2 Select Advanced Chipset Features. Press Enter.

3 At the next screen, select AGP and P2P Bridge Control.

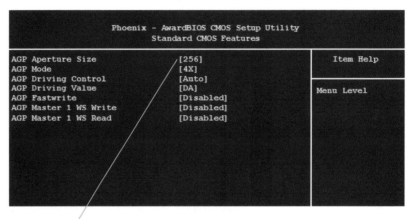

*The AGP Aperture Size setting determines how much of the system's memory the video adapter will use once its own built-in memory has been exhausted.*

4 Highlight AGP Aperture Size [256].

5 Use the Page up/Page down keys to select the [68] option.

6 Highlight AGP Mode and ensure the [X] matches that of your video adapter (8X, 4X, 2X. etc.). This will be in the documentation.

*Once you have found an AGP Aperture Setting that is compatible with your system, it's perfectly all right to leave it at that setting. So, you can give step 7 a miss if you don't want the bother of repeating steps 1 to 5 several times.*

7 Reboot, and your display should be restored. Repeat steps 1 to 5 to select the highest AGP Aperture Size your system can handle. (The usual recommended setting for this is half your system memory. So if you have 512 MB of memory in your system, you'd set this to 256). This isn't set in stone, however, so you can experiment a bit.

These instructions and screenshots were taken from a Phoenix 6.00 PG BIOS. Yours may vary somewhat.

If the display has been working OK and then suddenly goes blank after a period of inactivity, check the following:

## Advanced Power Management

*Advanced Power Management (APM) is a Windows feature that is designed specifically for the users of Laptop computers. It enables these users to configure power saving settings that enable the laptop's battery power to be conserved as much as possible. For example, the computer can be configured to switch itself to Standby mode after a specified period. Individual components, such as the hard drive and the monitor, can also be configured in the same way. This last setting can be the cause of a seemingly dead monitor.*

Advanced Power Management (APM) is a Windows application that allows the user to set a time, after which specific parts of their PC are placed in standby mode or switched off. In the case of a monitor this has the effect of blanking the screen. In theory, a slight movement of the mouse will bring the monitor back to life, but it doesn't always work like that; sometimes it can take a considerable amount of mouse clicking and key bashing to get the monitor back again. Make sure this isn't the cause of the problem before going any further. If necessary, reboot the PC to be sure.

*Unless you really are keen on watching fish swimming across your desktop, bouncing balls, starfields, etc, you really are well advised to disable screensavers.*

*These were originally designed to prevent "image burn," whereby static images were literally burnt into the monitor. Modern monitors are not susceptible to this problem and so there is really no need for them now.*

*They are also notorious for causing system crashes and slowdowns, particularly some of the 3D screensavers available for download from the Internet.*

To make sure an APM scheme hasn't been inadvertently enabled on your PC, right-click the Desktop and then click Properties, Screensavers, Settings. Now you can alter or disable the APM settings.

## Screensavers

Screensavers kick in after a set period. One of the screensaver options is Blank. If this has been selected, the display will do just that – go blank. Check this out as described below:

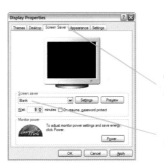

1  Right-click the Desktop and then click Properties.

2  Click the Screensaver tab.

3  Make sure the Blank option has not been selected.

# XP & Refresh Rates

Staring for hours at a display that is flickering very slightly, even if it is almost imperceptible, is guaranteed to eventually scramble your brains. This is an old problem that can occur with a CRT monitor, and is caused by the display's refresh rate being set too low.

Versions of Windows prior to XP automatically set the refresh rate to the highest rate that the monitor can handle, so this is rarely a problem with these systems.

This is not the case with XP, however. When XP is installed, for some reason it almost always decides to choose a refresh rate that is less than optimal. The result is screen flicker.

Check this out as follows:

Right-click the Desktop, select Properties, Settings, Advanced.

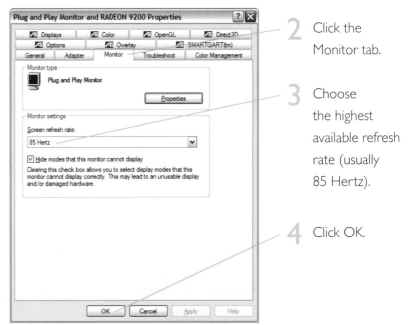

2 Click the Monitor tab.

3 Choose the highest available refresh rate (usually 85 Hertz).

4 Click OK.

The screen will now go blank for a few seconds before reappearing with a dialog box asking if you want to keep the new setting. Click Yes to accept the new refresh rate.

# Display Is Scrambled

*Certain video adapters can also cause a scrambled display when XP is run for the first time.*
*The solution is to reboot and select Enable VGA Mode in XP's Startup Options. When you're back in Windows, reinstall the video adapter driver, which should clear the problem.*

The screen is a unintelligible mass of lines. This problem occurs for two reasons:

- Incorrect Refresh Rate.

- Incorrect Screen Resolution.

The procedure for resolving both of the above is as follows:

1 Restart the PC and go to Startup Options by tapping the F8 key as the computer reboots.

2 Use the arrow keys to select Enable VGA Mode. Hit Enter.

*Video Graphics Array (VGA) is a basic video display system for PCs, which provides a screen resolution of 640 by 480 with 16 colors. All PCs are capable of using this system – because of this, it is useful when troubleshooting video problems.*

XP will now load a generic video driver, which will clear the scrambled display and thus allow you to find out what's causing the problem.

The first thing to try is setting a lower refresh rate, as described on page 82. Reboot the PC normally. If the problem is still present:

3 Repeat Steps 1 and 2 above.

4 Right-click the Desktop, and select Properties, Settings.

*If you wish to experiment with different screen resolutions, right-click the Desktop, select Properties, Settings, Advanced, Adapter and List All Modes. This will open a dialog box showing all the screen resolutions available on your system.*
*In general though, assuming you are using a 17-inch monitor, a resolution of 1024 x 768 will be about right. Any lower than this and the display will be too large, while a higher setting will result in a display that's too small.*

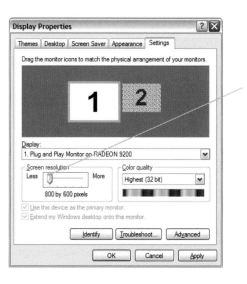

5 Reduce the Screen Resolution by dragging the slider to Less.

# Screen Redraws Slowly

This problem is most noticeable when graphics are being loaded, such as XP's Startup screen and dialog boxes. It is also apparent when scrolling down web pages.

This is quite a common issue and is the result of the video adapter driver having been uninstalled (intentionally or otherwise) or having become corrupted. In this situation XP takes over, and installs a basic VGA video driver (see page 83) that will work with all setups. However, while it will at least provide a picture, it will be slow. When a graphic is loaded, instead of appearing instantly, you can literally see it being drawn on the screen by the video system.

Check this out by right-clicking the Desktop and then clicking Properties, Settings, Advanced. Then click Adapter.

*Another way of checking your video adapter driver is by looking in XP's Device Manager. Details of the driver currently installed will be found under "Display Adapter."*

*You may also have a situation whereby the video driver shows up correctly in Step 1 opposite, but is nevertheless not working.*

*If this is the case it will almost certainly be corrupted. Check it out in the Device Manager to see if there are any reported problems. Otherwise, right-click the driver in the Device Manager and click Uninstall. Then reboot. On restart, XP will reinstall the driver.*

If there is nothing listed under Adapter Type then your video driver has been uninstalled or is corrupted.

2 Dig out your video adapter driver CD and place it in the CD drive.

3 Click the Properties button in the Adapter dialog box, the Driver tab and then Update Driver. The Add Hardware wizard will now open. Click Next and follow the steps in the wizard to reinstall the driver.

# The PC Won't Speak!

Your PC is not producing any sound. The first thing to establish is whether the problem applies to the whole system or just to parts of it.

Many PCs come with the sound system built into the mainboard. With this type of system the speakers need an independent power supply (the mains supply). If they are not plugged into the mains, they will not work. Usually, they will also have an on/off switch, which obviously needs to be in the "On" position.

First, try playing a music CD in the CD-ROM drive. If that doesn't work try playing a WAV file by going to Control Panel, Sounds and Audio Devices.

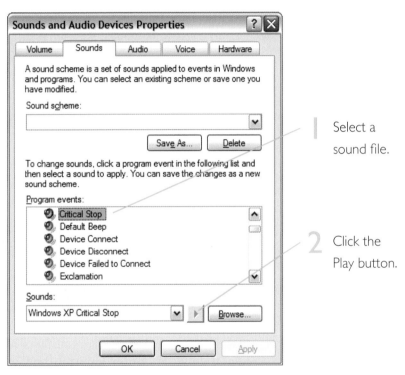

Select a sound file.

Click the Play button.

If the problem occurs after upgrading your system to Windows XP, then there is a good possibility that your sound card is not compatible with XP. You may need to obtain an updated driver from the manufacturer to get it working.

If either of these tests produces sound then the problem is not too serious, as they indicate that the sound card, speakers and speaker connections are all OK. The problem will be specific to a particular application. Reinstalling the application in question will usually fix the problem.

Make sure your speakers are connected to the correct socket. This is the "Speaker Out" or "Line Out" socket.

Also, check the volume control in Windows hasn't been turned down or muted. Check this out in Sounds and Audio Devices in the Control Panel.

If, however, you can't get any sound at all then you need to investigate further.

# Checking the Sound Card

*If you have recently installed the sound card on a system that was previously using the onboard sound system built into the mainboard, you may have to disable the onboard sound in the BIOS.*

*You will also need to relocate the speaker connections to the Line Out socket on the sound card.*

*Corrupted sound card drivers are one of the most common faults on a computer. Fortunately, this is a simple matter to rectify. You can simply reinstall the driver; alternatively, use System Restore to restore the computer to a date on which the sound system was working.*

*Check that Windows is configured to use your sound card. Do this as follows:*

1) *Open Device Manager.*

2) *Double-click Sound, video, and game controllers.*

3) *Double-click your sound device.*

4) *Click the Properties tab, and then double-click Audio Devices.*

5) *Click your sound device, and then click Properties.*

6) *Click Use audio features on this device.*

The next thing to check is that your sound card is correctly installed. Go to Start, Control Panel, Sounds and Audio Devices.

Click the Audio tab and you will see three sections – Sound playback, Sound recording and Midi music playback. If the first two are grayed out and have nothing listed under Default device, then the sound card driver is missing or corrupted.

If these two boxes are grayed out, it indicates that the sound card is not installed correctly.

If the sound card driver is not installed then run the Add Hardware wizard in the Control Panel to reinstall it.

In the unlikely event that you still have no sound after this, try checking for resource conflicts in Device Manager. Go to Start, Control Panel, System, Hardware, Device Manager. If your sound card is listed, there should be a colored symbol next to it. Double-click the entry, and the nature of the problem will be revealed in the next dialog box.

If it still doesn't work, check that the sound card is firmly seated in its socket on the mainboard. Finally, try installing a different card.

# General Sound Problems

### Jerky or Intermittent Sound

Stuttering or broken-up sound is usually a result of a lack of system memory (RAM), although the problem can also be caused by faulty speakers, cables or connections.

Check the amount of RAM available as follows:

*If you are using USB speakers, unplug all other USB devices and make sure the speakers are plugged directly into one of the PC's USB ports. This will eliminate any bandwidth drain on the USB channel that the other devices may be causing.*

1 Right click the Taskbar and select Task Manager.

2 Click the Performance tab.

*Jerky sound can also be caused by faulty or incompatible drivers, so be sure to check for updates. If you are already using the newest version, try the following:*

*1) Go to the Control Panel and click Sounds and Audio Devices.*

*2) On the Volume tab, under Speaker Settings, click the Advanced button.*

*3) Click the Performance tab and you'll notice two options: one for Hardware Acceleration and another for Sample Rate Conversions. Take both of them down a notch and see if the problem is fixed.*

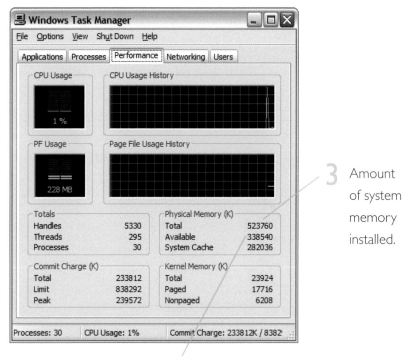

3 Amount of system memory installed.

4 Amount of system memory available.

If the amount of memory available to the system is low, then click the Processes tab on the Task Manager and quit any programs that are using a large amount of memory.

*Don't lose sight of the fact that the quality of most sound equipment supplied with PCs is usually of a low standard. This applies particularly to speakers and microphones. Don't expect to get high-quality results unless you are prepared to fork out for high-quality components.*

*When making recordings on your PC with a microphone, be aware that a computer does not provide the ideal environment for this type of application. For example, you may notice low-level noise in the background of your recording. This can be caused by the PC's disk drives and system fan.*

*Humming sounds can be caused by "ground loop." This occurs where there is more than one electrical path to ground. Tracing and eliminating the exact source of ground loop can be complicated, but light dimmer switches, motorized appliances, and cable TV outlets are prime suspects.*

## Distorted Sound

This problem can be caused by an excessively high volume level or a mismatch between speaker volume level and sound device volume level. Adjust these as follows:

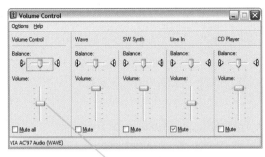

1 Turn the volume control on your speakers to its middle position.

2 Open the volume control by going to Start, Control Panel, Audio and Sound Devices. Click the Volume tab and then Advanced. Adjust the left-most volume slider to a comfortable level.

## CD/DVD Drive Has No Sound

If you find your CD/DVD drive is not producing any sound, do the following:

1 Go to Start, Control Panel, System, Hardware, Device Manager. Click the + sign next to DVD/CD-ROM Drives and then click your drive. Click the Properties tab.

*If you have a dedicated sound card in your system, check that the CD-ROM drive is connected to it. There should be a small three-wire cable with a four-pin socket that connects to the back of the drive unit. If the drive has recently been installed, this could have been overlooked.*

2 Make sure the Volume slider isn't set to Low.

# System Instability Troubleshooting

Computers are predictable and reliable machines, they do exactly what they are told and nothing more or less. There is no other way for them to be as they can react only to the instructions they are given. As long as the instructions are logical and do not conflict, and the operating conditions are within the designated parameters, the computer will perform exactly as it should.

However, tell it to do something that is impossible or illogical, or subject it to something it isn't designed to cope with – extreme heat for example – and all of a sudden that reliability disappears. The computer doesn't know how to react – things are happening that shouldn't be. In short, it has become unstable.

## Covers

Chapter Nine

# Strategy

*When your computer starts misbehaving – crashing and freezing – it's a sure sign that things are happening inside it that shouldn't be. Sort the problem out immediately, don't ignore it with the vague hope that it might sort itself out; what's more likely to happen is that the problem will get worse.*

When a computer becomes unstable, it starts behaving unpredictably. Typical symptoms include:

- Random error messages.

- Crashes, lock-ups and hanging.

- Generally unpredictable and unusual behavior.

Unfortunately, instability problems in a PC can be very difficult to pin down, as there are so many possible causes. Both hardware and software can be to blame, not to mention external factors such as heat and electrical interference. Even worse, these problems can be intermittent, making it difficult to know whether a particular troubleshooting step has worked or not.

*Don't forget the possibility that the problem might actually have nothing to do with the computer itself. External factors such as fluctuating power supplies, heat, and severe electrical interference can all have an impact on a computer's performance.*

*NOTE: in the event of close proximity lightning storms, isolate the computer completely. Many a PC has been well and truly "cooked" by lightning.*

The first thing to do is get as many clues as you can. Things to take note of are:

- Is the problem hardware- or software-related?

- Is the fault predictable – can you reproduce it?

- What applications were running at the time?

- Does it occur when running a specific program?

- Does it occur when using a specific hardware device such as a mouse or modem?

- Any changes to the computer setup immediately prior to the fault occurring, such as installing an application or device.

*When diagnosing instability issues, take time out to have a good think first. There are so many factors that could be involved, it's essential to narrow things down before you start troubleshooting.*

- Error messages.

- Have you been tinkering with settings or system components?

- When does the problem occur; for example, does it happen within a few minutes of starting up?

Going through the above list will help narrow the problem down and give you a starting point from which to locate the cause of the problem.

# Software Issues

*The first step is to establish if the fault is hardware- or software-related. If you can do this conclusively then you have immediately eliminated many potential causes.*

If you have worked through the list on the previous page and still have no idea of where to start, the first thing to do is to establish whether the fault is hardware- or software-related. Do this by rebooting into Safe Mode (see page 37) and see if the problem is still there. If it isn't then it's likely the problem has to do with your software, which is the cause of most instability problems.

Troubleshoot as follows:

### Switch Off

Switch the computer off and then restart it – this simple step will resolve many problems. It is important that you do this correctly though, using XP's Turn Off button. Using the power off switch or reset button can cause further problems.

*Before you do anything else, switch the computer off for about 20 seconds and then restart it. This action has been mentioned several times already in this book, but it bears repeating, particularly in relation to an unstable computer. Many causes of instability are transient in nature and can often be resolved by switching off. Also, don't forget to reboot the computer periodically to avoid the issue of RAM fragmentation.*

It is also important to reboot the PC at least once a day, otherwise your RAM will become fragmented by programs leaving bits of themselves in RAM when they are closed down. Over a period of time these fragments will build up and much of your RAM will be unusable. This is when you are likely to see the "Your system is dangerously low on resources" error message. Also, because the system is having to hunt around in RAM for the data it wants, everything is slowed down. This can cause instability.

### Running Applications

If the problem occurs when you are running several applications simultaneously, close down as many as you can. Too many open programs can overstretch your RAM as the various applications all compete for the available resources. Crashes and lock-ups are a common result.

*Avoid running 3D games in conjunction with other applications. These can cause even well specified machines to struggle at times, particularly if other programs are also open.*

### Screensavers

Screensavers are a common cause of crashes and general system instability, particularly the 3D type that use Microsoft's OpenGL technology. These are a black hole as far as system resources are concerned.

Many of the ones available for download from the Internet are also poorly coded and should be avoided. In general, the more complex the screensaver, the more likely it is to cause problems.

## Startup Programs

Disable all programs that start automatically with XP, many of which run invisibly in the background and can cause problems.

1 Go to Start, Run. In the Run box type MSCONFIG and press OK.

2 Click the System Configuration Utility's Startup tab.

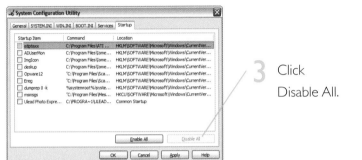

3 Click Disable All.

Reboot and see if the problem has now cleared. If it has, reenable the Startup programs one by one, rebooting each time until the problem reappears. The last program enabled will be the culprit.

## Adware/Spyware

Adware or spyware software is an extremely likely cause of system instability, particularly if you do a lot of downloading from the Internet. The main problem with these programs is that they are very often poorly coded, which can cause stability problems in the host computer. To get rid of them you need to scan your system with anti-spyware software such as "Ad-aware."

Adware and spyware are parasite programs, attached to legitimate programs, which install themselves surreptitiously on the PC. These programs may do any of the following:

- Record your surfing habits and sites visited.
- Record your spending habits and items bought.
- Steal credit card details and passwords.
- Extract email addresses.
- Hijack your browser.

## Advanced Power Management (APM)

APM is a Windows application that allows a PC to be switched off, or put on standby, after a designated period. It is really intended for use on laptop computers, where power conservation is an important issue. However, it is also found on desktop PCs and its use has been known to cause instability issues. Try disabling it:

Go to Start, Control Panel, Power Options.

2 Click the Power Scheme tab.

3 Select Never for all options.

## XP's Services

When stopping or disabling any of XP's services, remember to check for possible consequences. Double-click the service and then click the Dependencies tab. This will tell you what effect disabling the service will have on the system.

XP has a number of services, which are applications configured to run invisibly in the background and which control various XP functions.

If you experience instability problems when carrying out a particular task, CD burning for example, take a look at the Services dialog box and see if you can find one that relates to the task causing the problem.

These services can be disabled as follows:

Go to Start, Control Panel and click Administrative Tools.

If you do find that a particular service is causing problems, there will be no easy way to fix it; reinstalling XP will probably be the only solution. Alternatively, if you can live without it, just leave it disabled.

2 Click Services and scroll down to the service in question.

3 Double-click the service and you will see options to Stop and also to Disable. Click Disable and see if the problem has now cleared.

## Hard Drive Issues

One of the prerequisites for optimal system performance is sufficient available hard disk space. There are two reasons for this:

Firstly, when a disk is approaching its capacity, the effects of fragmentation (see page 54) are increased considerably. An inevitable consequence of this is slowdown of system performance and increased likelihood of crashes and lock-ups.

Secondly, the system's page file operates from the hard disk. This file is created by Windows as a RAM substitute, and is used when there is no more RAM available. Typically, XP's page file can be anything up to 1.5 GB, and if there is not sufficient room on the hard disk to accommodate it, the system will struggle when required to multitask.

So try creating more hard disk space by deleting unnecessary files or moving them to a different drive. Alternatively, you can configure the page file to operate from a separate hard drive or partition if you have one available – see page 99.

## Clogged Up System

"Clogged up" is not a particularly technical term, but it describes accurately enough a Windows installation that has been well used over a long period. The constant installation/uninstallation of applications, creation and deletion of files, accumulation of temporary files, junk from the Internet, and so on, will result in a PC that is literally clogged up with redundant data, cross linked files, invalid shortcuts, etc.

Such a system will inevitably suffer adversely in terms of performance and reliability. Niggling errors will build up and general system instability will creep in.

When faced with a computer in this state, the best thing to do is to scrub it clean and start again from scratch. To do this you first need to collect all the data and settings you wish to keep, and save them to a separate backup medium. Then reformat the hard disk (see pages 56–57), install a fresh copy of XP and then finally reinstall your data and settings. Simply reinstalling XP will cure only the niggles – you'll still have a clogged-up PC.

A hard disk drive that is running low on space is likely to result in an unstable system. If the drive is heavily fragmented as well, things will be even worse. The more you fill up your drive, the more pronounced the effects of fragmentation will be.

Defragment the drive on a weekly basis to keep it in good order. If you can't see yourself keeping to this, configure XP's Task Scheduler to do the job for you automatically as follows:

1) Go to Start, All Programs, Accessories and System Tools.

2) Click Scheduled Tasks.

3) Click the Browse button and go to the Windows folder on your hard drive. Open the System32 folder and scroll down to the file named defrg. Click this and then follow the instructions in the Scheduled Tasks wizard.

If you are really serious about keeping your system in tip-top order then you ought to periodically reformat your drive and then reinstall fresh copies of XP and your applications. Doing this will result in a PC that runs like new.

## Corrupted or Incompatible Drivers

Hardware drivers are one of the most common causes of system instability; particularly so with XP, given its dislike of incompatible drivers.

*A device driver is a small piece of software that acts as an interface between the device and Windows. Some drivers also act as an interface between the device and the user. For example, when you open your printer software to change some settings, what you are looking at is the driver.*

*Drivers have three purposes:*

*1) They "introduce" the associated device to Windows and tell it what the device requires in the way of system resources.*

*2) They allow the user to make changes to the device's settings, as in our printer example above.*

*3) They provide a method for manufacturers to update and increase the performance and capabilities of existing devices.*

Very often problems will occur directly after a driver installation. If this is the case, immediately uninstall the driver and see if the fault clears. If it does then you need to update the driver, as it clearly isn't compatible with XP. Visit the manufacturer's website and there should be an XP update available.

There is also the possibility that the driver is OK but is conflicting with another device. Check this out as follows:

1 Go to Start, Control Panel, System, Hardware, Device Manager.

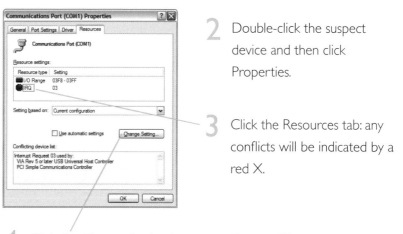

2 Double-click the suspect device and then click Properties.

3 Click the Resources tab: any conflicts will be indicated by a red X.

4 Click the Change Setting button to allocate different resources to the device.

Sometimes a driver will have been corrupted for some reason – an incorrect system shutdown, for example. (Sound card drivers are well known for this.) Simply reinstall it.

You can quickly establish if a particular driver is faulty by checking in the Device Manager. Problem devices are marked as such by colored symbols. Right-clicking the device in question and clicking Properties will usually tell you the nature of the problem.

# Hardware Issues

If you're satisfied the issue is not software-related, or following the software troubleshooting steps on the previous pages hasn't yielded results, then you'll need to look at the hardware side of things.

## Hard Disk Factors

Hard disk drives may, over a period of time, develop bad sectors. This can cause unpredictable computer behavior. XP comes with a built-in disk checking utility called Chkdsk, which will check for, and attempt recovery of, bad sectors. You will need to configure Chkdsk to do this though, as by default it will check and repair only file system errors. Do it as follows:

1 Go to Start, My Computer. Right-click the drive you want to check and select Properties.

2 Click the Tools tab and then click Check now.

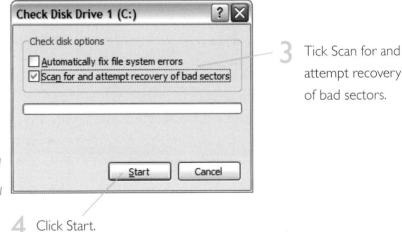

3 Tick Scan for and attempt recovery of bad sectors.

4 Click Start.

This can be a protracted procedure, particularly on a large disk drive, so if possible do it just before you turn in for the night. However, it is not something you need to do too often, especially if your disk drive is new – once every few months will suffice, unless of course your PC starts acting up.

*If you decide to install extra hardware on your PC, such as a dedicated video adapter or a TV tuner card, don't forget that you will also be raising the heat levels within the system case. While most systems should be able to cope with a couple of extra cards, any more than this could result in problems down the line.*

*Also bear in mind the possibility that the extra hardware may be making demands of the power supply that it cannot cope with. A blown power unit could be the result, and when power units blow they have a habit of also blowing the CPU, RAM chips and possibly the mainboard as well.*

*When upgrading, it might pay to also invest in a power supply unit with a higher power rating.*

*Another cause of system instability is a fluctuating power supply. This could be the mains supply itself or the PC's internal power supply.*

*If you suspect the mains supply could be the problem, fit a surge protector.*

*As regards the PC's power unit, unless you have suitable test equipment such as an oscilloscope, your only option is to replace it.*

## Eliminate Your Hardware

System instability can be caused by a faulty hardware device. Peripherals such as printers and scanners are unlikely to cause such problems, but video, sound, TV tuners and network devices definitely can. If this is the case, the faulty device will need to be removed; if you don't know which it is, you will need to remove them all (with the exception of the video adapter) and then reinstall them one by one until the fault reappears.

Before you start physically removing your hardware devices though, you can try disabling them in Windows via the Device Manager:

1 Go to Start, Control Panel, System, Hardware, Device Manager.

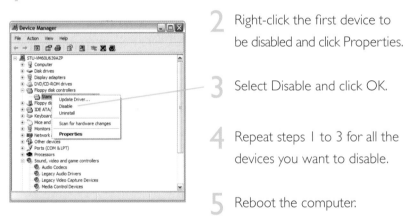

2 Right-click the first device to be disabled and click Properties.

3 Select Disable and click OK.

4 Repeat steps 1 to 3 for all the devices you want to disable.

5 Reboot the computer.

If the problem is still there then you will have to do it the hard way by physical removal: this is the only conclusive way to do it.

## Heat

A computer is a machine and, like all machines, must operate within designated parameters. These include heat, an excess of which is a PC's arch enemy. Apart from eventually causing individual components to fail, excess heat in the system case will cause all manner of faults. So what can cause heat to build up?

The main culprit is dust (an insulator). Over time this will build up in a layer over the circuit boards and also clog up the air circulation vents at the rear of the case. When this happens the inside of the case will overheat. To prevent this, periodically blow away the dust with a can of compressed air.

# Troubleshooting & Installing RAM

RAM modules are very sensitive to electrostatic electricity. You must ground yourself before touching them. This also applies to all the circuit boards in your computer. Handle them only by the edges if possible.

You will find available for download on the Internet any number of free memory diagnostic programs, including one from Microsoft. Typically, these create a diagnostic floppy disk.

Locate the Microsoft version by typing "Microsoft memory diagnostic software" into any search engine. You will find a number of sites offering the download.

Frequent system crashes accompanied by the notorious "blue screen of death" are a sure sign of a faulty RAM module. If this is the case you will have no other option but to replace it. With a bit of luck, however, you may have two RAM modules in your system. If so, remove one of them and see if the problem clears. If it doesn't, replace it and remove the other one.

NOTE: RAM modules are extremely sensitive to the electrostatic electricity that is present in your body. Before touching them you must ground yourself – touching the metal chassis of the case will do.

Having established that you require a new RAM chip, you now need to make sure you get the right one. This is not as straightforward as it may seem, due to the proliferation of various types – DIMMs, SIMMs, DDR, etc. Relevant details might be in the manual if you're lucky, or you could try contacting the manufacturer. While you will no doubt get some advice, don't forget that PC manufacturers make many different models and you could well find you are given the wrong advice and end up buying something that is useless to you. Will they offer to recompense you – well, what do you think? Probably the safest option is to take the faulty module to a computer store and ask for a straight swap.

When it comes to fitting your new RAM module you need to follow the same rules as when you removed the original – ground yourself well, particularly if you are standing on a carpet.

Apart from being somewhat intricate, the actual installation of the module is quite straightforward. Make sure the two retaining clips are opened out and then maneuver the module in place. It should slip in quite easily.

However, if you find yourself trying to force the retaining clips to engage then stop immediately – the module either isn't seated correctly or is the wrong type. Whatever you do, don't try and force it in place, you'll probably end up damaging the mainboard. Confirm you have the correct type before going any further.

Once installed, reboot, and at the first boot screen you'll see the memory count. If this is correct then you're up and running.

# XP's Page File

*You can of course use XP's installation disk to create a partition for the page file, as described on pages 56–57. However, unlike Partition Magic, which can create a partition without destroying existing data, XP can create a partition only in unallocated space. If there is none, it has to take space from an existing partition. In the process it will destroy that partition and all the data on it. Put simply, you will have to start again from scratch – create and format your partitions and then install a new copy of XP.*

The page file (also known as the swap file) is a file created by Windows to be used when the system is running out of physical memory (RAM). Typically, the need for this occurs when the installed amount of RAM is low or the user is running a number of applications simultaneously.

To keeps things chugging along, Windows creates this file on the hard disk drive and uses it as a RAM substitute. However, if Windows cannot find enough room on the disk to create the page file then the system can slow to a crawl and also become very unstable.

Another problem can be caused by fragmentation. Over time the hard disk becomes fragmented, as we saw on page 54. This also applies to the page file, thus slowing the computer even more.

However, if you use a separate disk or partition specifically for the page file, as described below, both of these problems can be avoided.

*Even better than creating a specific partition for the Paging file, is to put it on a second hard disk. This is because the beginning of a hard disk is the area that gives the fastest data transfer rate. If you decide to do this, format the drive first and then create the Page file before you put anything else on the drive. This ensures the Page file will be at the beginning of the disk, and so its performance will be as fast as possible.*

1　Go to Start, Control Panel, System, Advanced, Performance Settings, Advanced, Virtual Memory. Click the Change button.

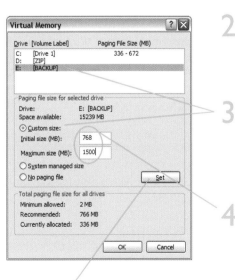

2　Disable the original page file by highlighting drive C and ticking No paging file.

3　Highlight the drive or partition you want to use for the new page file and then tick Custom size.

4　Enter the page file sizes in the boxes (768 & 1500).

5　Click Set and OK. Reboot for the changes to take effect.

# Instability Error Messages

There are far too many messages to be able to list them all, so we will concentrate on the ones most likely to crop up.

It must be pointed out here that while the error messages detailed in this section were all quite common with previous versions of Windows, due to XP's inherent stability these messages are now relatively rare. That said, they do still occur from time to time.

It's also worth remembering that the vast majority of stability problems are temporary in nature and can be resolved by the simple expedient of switching off and then on again. So always try this first.

## General Protection Faults

A General Protection Fault occurs when a program tries to access a part of the system memory (RAM) that is already in use.

One of Windows's main purposes as an operating system is to provide memory to an application that is requesting it. If the memory it allocates is already occupied by another program, a General Protection Fault will be the result. Windows will then close down the program; the error itself will not do any damage. The problem is that Windows forces you out of your program, so anything not previously saved is lost.

So what can you do when you persistently get this type of fault?

The first thing is to ensure you have enough available hard drive space and RAM. Insufficient memory is the most common cause of General Protection Faults.

Next, run a defragmenting utility on your hard drive.

Disable any screensavers you may have running. These are a common cause of crashes, which is what a General Protection Fault basically is.

Close any programs that may be running in the background. Reduce your desktop color depth as described on page 83. For example, if it is currently set to 32 bits, try lowering it to 16 bits. The lower the color depth, the less the resources being used. You can also try lowering your screen resolution.

*An exception error signifies that something unexpected has happened within the Windows environment, typically an improper memory access; for example, an application or a Windows component reading or writing to a memory location that has not been allocated to it, thus overwriting and corrupting other program code in that area of memory.*

*When an exception error occurs, the processor returns an exception to the operating system; this exception is handled as a fatal exception error. In many cases, the exception is nonrecoverable, and the system must be restarted or shut down, depending on the severity.*

## Fatal Exception Errors

These are very similar to General Protection Faults in that they can be caused by two applications trying to access the same section of RAM simultaneously. Device drivers are common villains in this respect.

However, they can also be caused by a fault in your system's hardware, such as a defective RAM module. Faulty CPUs can also cause Fatal Exception Errors. These messages are usually displayed on a blue screen – the so-called "Blue Screen of Death."

To resolve persistent Fatal Exceptions you must reboot into Safe Mode (see page 37). This will establish if the cause of the problem lies in your software or hardware.

If it is software-related (indicated by the problem going away in Safe Mode), then the culprit is quite likely to be the program you were running when the error occurred. Try reinstalling it. Then check out your device drivers in Device Manager.

If, however, the problem is still present in Safe Mode, then it will be something to do with your hardware. The most likely cause will be a faulty RAM chip. You could also have a failing or overheated CPU.

*Only those parts of a program and data that is currently in active use need to be held in physical RAM; other parts are placed in the page file. When a program tries to access an address that is not currently in physical RAM, it generates an interrupt that asks the system to retrieve the page containing that address from the page file. Sometimes, however, through software or hardware error, the page is not in the page file either: the system then produces an Invalid Page Fault error.*

## Invalid Page Faults

Invalid Page Fault errors occur when Windows runs out of RAM and attempts to use virtual memory (the page file) but is unable to do so for some reason.

1. Optimize your hard drive by running Chkdsk to check for damaged sectors, as described on page 96.

2. Check your RAM modules by replacing them with ones known to be good – see page 98.

3. Make sure your hard disk has at least 1.5 GB of free space to accommodate XP's swap file.

If all else fails, then as a last resort reinstall Windows – see page 40.

*Whenever XP is presented with something that it can't process or resolve, it generates an illegal operation error message.*

*User error is the most common cause of illegal operation error messages. For example, whenever an older program, or one that was not designed for XP (such as a printer or scanner driver) is installed, you run a risk of corrupting XP. This is why XP will show you a warning message when you install an uncertified driver.*

*Windows Protection Error messages are usually seen when you start or shut down Windows, and can be caused by any of the following:*

*• Conflicts between real-mode and protected-mode drivers.*

*• A damaged Registry.*

*• A virus*

*• A damaged WIN.COM or COMMAND.COM file.*

*• CMOS settings errors.*

*• Plug and Play malfunction.*

*• Hardware faults, such as malfunctioning RAM or a faulty mainboard.*

## Illegal Operations

These are probably the most common error messages of all and are usually specific to a particular application. For this reason they are also the easiest to resolve. In the vast majority of cases, simply uninstalling and then reinstalling the program running when the error occurred will fix the problem.

## Windows Protection Errors

These errors are usually a result of an essential device driver not loading properly when Windows boots up. They are most likely to occur when a hardware device has been installed or changes have been made to the system.

First, reboot into Safe Mode and uninstall any devices that may have just been installed. Reboot and, if the problem has now cleared, try reinstalling the device.

Next, go into Device Manager and check for resource conflicts.

Run a virus checker on your system. Viruses can sometimes cause these errors, especially if the Windows system files are infected.

You may have a faulty RAM chip. Check by replacing with a good RAM module.

Finally, do a clean installation of Windows – see pages 56–57.

If none of these steps solves the problem then you almost certainly have a problem with your mainboard.

## Insufficient Memory Errors (or similar)

These error messages crop up when a program is shut down but fails to release all the memory it was occupying. Subsequent applications will thus not have enough memory available for them to run.

The solution is simple. Shut down the PC and then reboot. This action will clear the memory.

# Dealing With a Frozen PC

*If your computer stops responding for some reason, give it a few moments before hitting Ctrl+Alt+Del. This will open the Task Manager, through which you should be able to sort the problem out.*

When presented with a frozen or hung PC, many people will immediately hit the reset button. While this will certainly unfreeze the PC, it can, however, also lead to further problems such as file corruption.

When in this situation, exercise some patience. It could be that XP will sort the problem given a little time. Wait a few moments and then, if nothing seems to be happening, hit Ctrl+Shift+Esc simultaneously to bring up XP's Task Manager. Here you will be able to see if the problem is being caused by a particular program.

*Sometimes, applications have an extremely irritating habit of insisting on taking their time to close down. When this happens a dialog box will appear prompting the user to either end it now or to wait. The following tip will force XP to automatically close down the offending program.*

*1) Go to Start and click the Run box. Type REGEDIT.*

*2) In the registry, locate the following key: HKEY_USERS\ DEFAULT\Control Panel\ Desktop*

*3) In the right-hand window, locate AutoEndTasks.*

*4) Right-click AutoEndTasks, select Modify, and in the Value data box, enter "1"*

*5) Reboot for the change to take effect.*

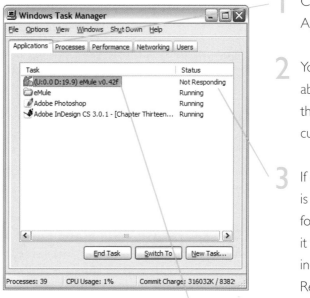

1 Click the Applications tab.

2 You will now be able to see all the applications currently open.

3 If one of them is responsible for the problem it will be indicated as Not Responding.

4 Highlight the offending application and then click End Task.

Nine times out of ten, XP will manage to close the non-responding program and thus unfreeze the computer. Sometimes, however, even this won't work, and it's at this point that you may have to resort to the reset button. If you do, make sure that Chkdsk is run on restart to correct any problems that this may have caused.

# Keeping Your PC Stable

Not only will the tips on this page help to keep your PC stable, they will also have a positive effect on its overall performance.

### Defragment Your Disk Drive On a Regular Basis

Many people will run a PC for years and will defragment rarely, if ever; the consequence of this will be a heavily fragmented drive that will have a major impact on overall performance, not to mention instability issues. Do it regularly, as described on page 54.

### Scan for Viruses

The Internet is rife with viruses. All downloads are potentially dangerous. Scan them all with an up-to-date virus checker. The same applies to incoming emails.

Be particularly wary of downloading freeware/shareware software; many will contain bugs that can cause problems, plus unwelcome attachments in the form of spyware and adware (see page 147).

### Update Your Device Drivers

Keeping your drivers current is particularly important given that XP, more so than any previous version of Windows, is so unforgiving of incompatible or outdated hardware. All major manufacturers will have XP-rated drivers for their products available for free download.

### Don't Overuse Your Hard Disk

A hard disk that is at or near the limits of its capacity will not perform well. It will be sluggish and prone to errors. Keep at least 20 percent of its capacity free.

### Anti-Virus Software/Disk Management Utilities

Anti-virus software is best used only when needed. Leaving all options permanently enabled will have a serious impact on system performance. Run it to check your downloads and emails and then close it down. The same applies to disk management software. These types of applications can seriously slow your system down.

### Keep It Lean & Mean

The more applications you have installed, the greater the potential for things to go wrong. Install only the programs you need and get rid of the rest.

Periodically, run XP's Disk Cleanup utility. You will find this in System Tools on the All Programs menu.

Use this to get rid of redundant data such as temporary Internet files, temp files and setup files.

If you want a trouble-free operating environment, don't be tempted to try a dual/multi-boot setup. While these can work quite well, they can also cause serious problems such as refusal to boot and even loss of data.

Even if you carry out all the steps on this page, your PC will eventually begin to struggle. Applications will take longer and longer to open, irritating little faults will develop and instead of being a pleasure to use, it will become a pain.

It's at this stage you need to get your mop and bucket out and give the thing a good clean. By this we mean a clean installation of Windows, as described on pages 56–57.

When you have done this, you will be amazed at how much more responsive the machine has become. Consider doing this once a year.

# Peripheral Troubleshooting

Of all the various types of peripheral, printers are probably the ones most likely to cause problems. We will see how to deal with the issues that typically afflict these devices.

Scanners are another popular add-on and bring their own set of problems. As with printers, these are mostly software issues and are not too difficult to resolve.

Digital Cameras are becoming very popular these days and we include a page on how to solve typical problems.

Even the humble mouse gets a look-in.

## Covers

**Chapter Ten**

# Printer Doesn't Print

There are quite a few things that can prevent a printer from working, most of which are fairly straightforward to put right. When faced with problems printing, absolutely the first thing to do is to ascertain whether the problem is a physical fault with the printer itself.

### Printer Test Page

All printers have the facility to print a test page, which is done with the printer isolated from the computer. This typically involves disconnecting the printer interface cable from the computer and then pressing a combination of buttons; the procedure varies from printer to printer.

*Assuming a software problem, the first thing to try when a printer refuses to work, is to simply switch it off and then on again. This will clear its memory and possibly reset whatever it was that was causing the problem. If this doesn't have any effect, try rebooting the PC. It won't always work, but often it can have the desired effect.*

If this test is successful, it establishes that the printer itself is OK and that the fault is related to either the software or the connections. For instructions on how to carry out a printer test, refer to the instructions in your printer's documentation.

### Does It Have Any Ink?

If the printer doesn't print the test page then you have a problem with the printer itself. Before rushing it off to the repair shop though, check the obvious: Is the ink cartridge empty? Most printer software will indicate the level of ink remaining, but this is by no means to be relied upon. A physical check is more reliable – take the cartridge out and have a close look at it. Also, run the nozzle/head cleaning utility, in case the print nozzles are clogged-up.

*All printers use a specially designated port called LPT1. If your printer is not configured to use this port, it won't work.*

*Check this out by going to the Control Panel and clicking Printers and Faxes. Right-click the Printer icon and select Properties. Click the Ports tab, and if LPT1 hasn't been selected then tick its associated checkbox.*

1 Go to Start, Control Panel, Printers and Faxes. Right-click the Printer icon, click Properties and then click the Utilities tab.

2 Click Head Cleaning to clear the ink nozzles.

## Printer Connections

Assuming the test page does print as it should, the next thing to check is that the printer cables are OK and connected to the correct ports. It is unlikely that there will be anything wrong with the printer interface cable, but do check that the connections to both the printer and the PC are sound.

A potential cause of problems is when you have your printer connected to the computer via another device, such as a scanner or Zip drive. Any problems with the device could also prevent the printer receiving data from the PC. Eliminate this possibility by connecting the printer directly to the computer.

## Is the Printer Installed?

Go to Start, Control Panel and click Printers and Faxes.

*Having your printer connected to the system via another device such as a Zip drive is fine as long as nothing goes wrong with the secondary device. If it does, you may find the printer doesn't work either.*

*If the printer appears to be having physical difficulty in printing – the paper is jamming, or it is making peculiar noises, have a look at the bottom of the paper feed tray. There is a good possibility that a foreign object has found its way in there.*

*If you have more than one printing device installed on the computer, it is quite possible that one of these has set itself as the default printer. Check this out in the Printers and Faxes applet in the Control Panel.*

*Note that some software applications will install a "virtual" printer on to the system. An example of this is Microsoft Office 2003, which will install the Microsoft Office Document Image Writer.*

1 If your printer is installed you will see it here.

2 Make sure it is configured as the default printer; this is indicated by the tick mark above it.

3 If it isn't set as default, click the printer.

4 Click the Printer menu and select Set As Default Printer.

If the printer isn't installed, insert its driver CD and install it via the Add Hardware wizard in the Control Panel.

Having eliminated the printer and its connections and ascertained it is correctly installed, you now know the problem is software-related. The first thing to check is that you haven't simply "Paused" the printer. Do this as follows:

1 Go to Control Panel, Printers. Click your printer and then click the Printer menu.

Have you tried cancelling any print jobs in the Windows Print Manager? One of these may not be responding, and thus will be preventing the printer from working.

*If the Print Manager is active in the system tray, click it, right-click any print jobs and then click Cancel.*

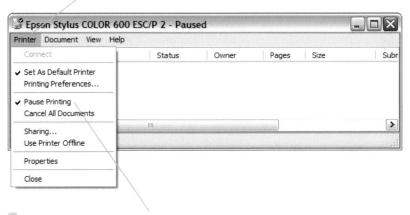

2 Make sure that the printer hasn't been Paused.

## Print Program

Problems with the spool file can prevent a printer from printing. (The spool file is a buffer, created on the hard disk, to which all print jobs are sent for queuing. This process can help speed up printing.) Eliminate this possibility by opening your printer software and selecting the "Print Directly to Printer" option.

Next, establish that the fault isn't being caused by the program that you are printing from – your word processor, for example. Do this by trying a different program, such as Wordpad or Notepad. Open up one of these, type a few lines, and then see if it prints; if it does then the program you were using originally is faulty and needs to be reinstalled.

## Resource Conflicts

The printer may have a resource conflict with another device. Check this out by going to Control Panel, System, Hardware, Device Manager, Ports (COM & LPT), Printer Port (LPT1). Right-click LPT1, click Properties, and, in the Printer Port Properties dialog box, click the Resources tab. In the Conflicting Device list at the bottom of the dialog box, check there are no problems.

# Printing is Slow

*If the document to be printed contains graphics, printing will inevitably be slow. This is particularly so if the print quality setting is set to high or finest.*

The most common cause of slow printing is the size of the file being printed. This is almost always because the document contains graphics, which can be enormous in size. If the computer's memory isn't large enough to cope with the volume of data being sent to it, or is already occupied by other applications, printing speed will be compromised.

There are two solutions to this problem:

- Decrease the size of any graphics in the document.

- Increase the amount of available memory.

There are two ways to reduce the size of an image file:

Firstly, reduce its resolution and color depth. This is easily achieved with an imaging program, such as Paint Shop Pro or IrfanView.

Secondly, save the image in a compressed image format such as JPEG. This can also be done in the same imaging program.

*Here are some other things you can do to speed up your printing:*

*1) Don't use color unless you have to. Color printing is much slower than black or grayscale.*

*2) Use Draft mode unless you need high-quality output.*

*3) Avoid rotated or resized bitmaps in your documents.*

*4) Use as few fonts as possible.*

Resizing and color depth reduction options in IrfanView.

*If you do, or plan to do, a lot of image-intensive printing, and you are having problems with your existing setup, a RAM upgrade will perform wonders with your printing speed; see page 98.*

You must also do everything you can to increase the amount of memory available to the printing operation. The best way to do this is simply to reboot (which will clear the PC's memory) and then to make sure no other programs are running.

If you carry out both of the above steps you should have no printing speed problems unless your machine is seriously under-specified to begin with (in which case you will need to upgrade it).

# Print Quality is Poor

### Print Nozzles

Typical symptoms are gaps or faint areas in the printed document, poor quality color, white horizontal lines, or even no print output at all.

*Another good reason for using your printer regularly is that many ink-jet printers will automatically run the nozzle cleaning utility after a prolonged period of inactivity.*

*As well as contaminating the platen, this cleaning process uses a considerable amount of ink. As ink-jet cartridges are expensive, you don't want to be wasting ink in this fashion.*

The reason is that the nozzles have become blocked, or partly blocked, by dried ink. Blocked nozzles are likely to be encountered in printers that haven't been used for a while. You can prevent this from happening by using the printer regularly, even if it's only to print a few words every other day.

If the nozzles are blocked, run the Head Cleaning utility from the printer software; this will be found under the Utilities tab.

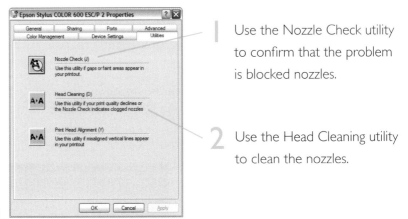

1 Use the Nozzle Check utility to confirm that the problem is blocked nozzles.

2 Use the Head Cleaning utility to clean the nozzles.

*Sometimes, if the nozzles are severely blocked, you will find you may need to run the head cleaning utility several times before the print quality is up to scratch. This is another good reason to run the printer regularly.*

### Keep The Printer Clean

Allowing the printer to get dirty is guaranteed to eventually adversely affect the quality of your printed documents. Although the print quality itself won't be affected, it can detract from the finished document in the form of smudges and streaks. Use a brush or can of compressed air to clear away general dust and dirt from the inner workings of the printer.

*Be wary of printing immediately after cleaning the printing heads. Very often the cleaning process will deposit ink on the printers platen, which will then be picked up by the document as it is being printed, resulting in streaks and marks. Make sure the platen is clean before you start printing.*

Another cause of spoiled print output is the nozzle cleaning utility, which works by forcing ink through the nozzles to clear them. It's not uncommon for the printer's platen (roller) to become contaminated with ink in this way, which will then be transferred to the document causing unsightly streaks. If this happens you will have to clean the ink off with a suitable solvent.

## Printer Software Settings

Another cause of low-quality printing is the selection of unsuitable settings in the printer software. For example, choosing economy print resolution (about 180 dots per inch [dpi]) will result in a faint print output. For high-quality printing you need 720 dpi or above. The drawback, of course, is that the higher the dpi setting, the slower the print speed. Also, the printer will use a lot more ink.

*Before printing, you need to select the correct type of paper for the particular application. When printing out photos, for example, you need to use photo-quality glossy paper.*

1 For good-quality printing you need to select suitable settings in the printer software.

2 If you want finer control over the settings, click the Advanced button.

Incorrect media selection can also cause problems. For example, if you try to print out a color photo on plain paper, the result will be less than impressive, as the colored ink will bleed into the absorbent paper; you need to use special glossy paper for this purpose. Also, it's no good choosing the right kind of paper and then hoping the printer will correctly guess what it is – it won't. You need to select it in the printer software.

3 Tell the printer what type of paper you are using.

# Ink-Jet Refills – Are They Worth It?

Branded ink-jet cartridges are well overpriced; because of this, a whole new industry has developed in which companies can seriously undercut the printer manufacturers and still show a profit. However, many people have had unhappy results with ink refill kits, so the jury is still out as to their worth.

## Pros

The main advantage of these kits is the price – a typical kit costs about the same as a branded cartridge, while offering about five times the amount of ink.

Another plus is convenience – if your cartridge gives up in the middle of the night and you have to get the document finished by morning, supplies will be at hand.

## Cons

Most of these kits involve injecting the ink into the cartridge with a syringe. As many people have discovered, this can be a very messy business indeed. It is also common for the refilled cartridge to leak while in use, which can result in the need for constant printer cleaning.

Using any old ink will not do – inks need to be formulated according to the brand of cartridge. Put the wrong type of ink in your cartridge and it might well not work at all. There is also the issue of ink quality. Predictably, the printer manufacturers claim that the quality of ink supplied with refill kits is inferior to their own and this is undoubtedly true in many cases. However, due to the huge profits to be made in the ink-jet market, many reputable companies have been set up that do supply a quality product: the problem is identifying them.

In an effort to discourage the refill practice, some printer companies have led consumers to believe that using refill kits will void printer warranties. This simply isn't true. A company may legally charge for any printer repairs caused by a refilled cartridge, but it must honor the warranty for other types of repair.

It is a fact, though, that millions of people are now using these kits and the consensus seems to be that, as long as you use a kit from a reputable supplier, you will get good results. Just don't forget to use a lot of newspaper when refilling your cartridge.

*If you don't wish to get your hands dirty, you can take your empty cartridges to specialist stores where the cartridge will be filled for you.*

*Don't be taken in by claims that your printer warranty will be voided by using refill kits: this is the printer manufacturers trying to protect their market. Obviously, they will not be liable for any damage resulting from the use of these kits, but they must honor the warranty for any non-related faults.*

*Ink-jet cartridge print heads have a limited lifespan. Even if you can refill your cartridge successfully, you will eventually have to junk it and buy a new one. The time to do this will be when your print quality becomes unacceptable.*

# Scanner Doesn't Scan

*Another common problem with scanners is that of initialization. This situation will be indicated by an error message. To resolve this issue you need to reboot the computer while the scanner is switched on. This action initializes the scanner's internal settings. On restart, the scanner will work.*

Scanners are essentially simple devices with little to go wrong inside them. If yours doesn't work, there are two likely problems:

- A corrupted or missing driver.
- The scanner has not been initialized.

If there is a problem with the driver, you will get an error message when you attempt to scan a file into your scanning software. This will be similar to that shown below:

*Those of you with USB scanners should be aware that USB requires a driver to enable it to function. So if you get a "Scanner not found" error message when you attempt a scan, this is the first thing for you to check. Go into Device Manager and at the bottom you will see a Universal Serial Bus Controllers category. Any problems with your USB driver will be indicated there.*

1 The message is telling you that no scanner has been found. This almost always means that the driver is missing or corrupt.

Check this out by going into the Device Manager.

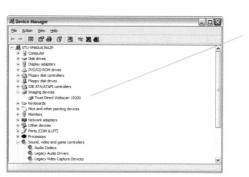

2 If your scanner is installed, it will be listed under Imaging Devices. In this situation there will usually be an exclamation mark next to it.

3 If there is, right-click the device, select Properties and you will see a dialog box that will tell you the nature of the problem.

It's more likely, though, that the scanner will not be listed at all, which means it hasn't been installed. Dig out the driver disk and install it with the Add Hardware wizard in the Control Panel.

# Scanner Issues

## Scans are Very Slow

Some scanners operate much more quickly than others, so establish that yours isn't one of the laggards before ripping it apart or taking it back to the store. Reading a few reviews of your model on the Internet should provide a few clues.

*Don't give too much credence to the scanner manufacturers' advertising claims of scan resolutions as high as 9,600 dpi. Scanners simply aren't capable of picking up this level of detail.*

*What the manufacturers are really referring to is something known as interpolation, which is a process that the scanning software uses to increase the perceived resolution of an image. It does this by creating extra pixels in between the ones actually scanned in. In short, it's basically guesswork and serves no practical purpose. If your scanner is capable of 600 dpi, that's all you will ever need.*

Assuming an abnormally slow scan, though, the usual reason is that the image is being scanned in at too high a resolution. This means the scan heads are having to read large amounts of data, which will, of course, slow down the scan. In the scanner software, lower the scan resolution. 300 dpi is more than enough for most applications; in many cases even that is overkill.

*Setting the scan resolution to 300 dpi or less will keep the image file small, and so speed up the scanning process.*

*Unless you are into top-end graphics work, a scan resolution of 300 dpi is more than enough for the vast majority of applications. If you're scanning a photo for a web page, for example, 75 dpi is ample.*

## A Scanned Image File Takes Ages to Open

This happens for the same reason as above – the image has been scanned in at too high a resolution. It's beyond the scope of this book to get into detail on this subject, but in the vast majority of cases it is absolutely unnecessary to use a resolution above 300 dpi. The result will be literally indistinguishable from that at a higher resolution, while the image file size will be tiny in comparison.

To illustrate this point, a page of text scanned in at 300 dpi results in an image file of approximately 900 kB, while the same page scanned at 600 dpi gives an image file of some 3.50 MB – nearly four times as big. However, in terms of clarity, the two images will be virtually indistinguishable.

Another cause can be a system low in RAM. If, for whatever reason, you must scan at the highest possible resolution, you may find that you have to upgrade your system's RAM capacity.

Having other applications running at the same time as the scan is in progress reduces the amount of memory available to the scanner, thus potentially slowing things down.

## Smudged or Marked Images

It is essential to ensure that the glass scanning surface inside the scanner is spotlessly clean. Any dirty marks or foreign bodies on it will be scanned in as part of the image. Clean the glass with a cloth prior to making the scan.

## Scanned Image is Not an Accurate Representation

Sometimes a scanned image looks somewhat different to the original picture – it might be a lot darker, for example. This is caused by an inherent weakness found in many scanners – poor gamma translation. Gamma is the term used as a measure of the brightness of mid-level tones in an image.

The problem can be corrected by using the Gamma Correction control found in any good imaging program.

*A phenomenon known as "moiré" can be an issue when scanning a newspaper or magazine photograph. This manifests itself as a herringbone pattern of interference.*

*Most scanner software will have a moiré control (sometimes called descreening). You can also try different scan resolutions to minimize the effect.*

*Most flatbed scanners are based on CCD (charged coupled device) technology. There is an inherent weakness in a CCD when it comes to capturing shadow detail. This is displayed as a general lack of contrast and definition in the shadow areas, causing them to become overly dark or lost altogether. This problem can be rectified with an imaging program's Gamma Correction control.*

*Most scanner software will also have a gamma control, which allows a user to adjust the gamma levels before the image is scanned. Initially this will be a trial and error process until the correct settings are reached. Once done, though, the setting can be set as default and all future scans will be correct in this respect.*

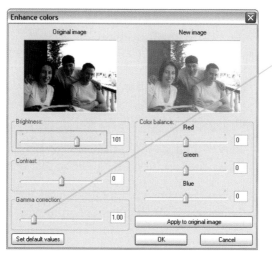

Gamma Correction control in IrfanView.

## Part of Scanned Image Missing

All scanner software includes a Preview mode, which allows you to select or crop the part of the image you want to scan in. If, after the scan has completed you find that part of your image is missing, it will be because you have cropped it out.

*Remember to check that all of the document to be scanned has been selected, by using the Preview function in your scanning software.*

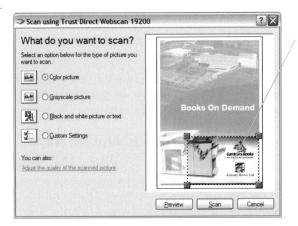

In this example, only the part of the document within the rectangle will be scanned.

## Garbled or Missing Text Characters

When a scanned text document is imported into a word processor, it needs to first go through a process known as Optical Character Recognition (OCR). This converts the image file into a text file that the word processor can recognize. OCR programs are supplied with all scanners.

*One of the most common uses of a scanner is to scan text documents into a word processor. For this to work, you will need an OCR program. However, these applications aren't perfect and will make mistakes.*

*Furthermore, just as with everything else, some OCR applications are better than others. In general, the OCR software supplied with scanners is not usually of the best quality. If you want or need really good results, then you will have to pay for one of the top-end packages, such as Scansoft's Omnipage Pro.*

Unfortunately, OCR software doesn't always produce perfect results – it makes the occasional mistake. While good OCR software can be 99% accurate, this will still result in several errors on any one page of text.

This is the first thing to be aware of – it isn't a fault as such, but rather the result of a technology that hasn't been perfected yet.

The performance of any OCR package basically comes down to the clarity of the text being scanned in. The more defined it is, i.e. dark characters on a white background, the better the result.

Similarly, small characters will be more difficult for the OCR program to read accurately. Also, the characters must be uniform – handwritten text will produce nothing but gibberish.

# Digital Cameras & Your PC

*Enable USB on your system as follows:*
*Go into the systems BIOS setup program, where there is an option for enabling/disabling USB.*

*Enter the BIOS, as described on page 51, and use the arrow keys to scroll down to Integrated Peripherals. Press Enter and scroll down to Onchip PCI Device. Press Enter again and you should now see the Onchip USB Controller option. Enable it, save your settings, and exit the BIOS.*

## Connections

One of the main problems users seem to experience with digital cameras is making a connection between the camera and the PC. To facilitate this, cameras are supplied with a data transfer lead. When digicams first came on the market, the serial port connection method was the one employed. These days, however, virtually all digital cameras use USB connections (due to their speed and ease of use) and so this is the method we will concentrate on.

Firstly, make sure USB is enabled on your PC, as described in the margin note. If USB is enabled but your camera is not showing in My Computer, then there is a problem with the USB driver.

1 Go to Control Panel, System, Hardware, Device Manager.

2 Expand the Universal Serial Bus Controller category.

*Before a digital camera will download to a computer, it must be switched on. Don't overlook this obvious step. Also, some cameras need to be set to a specific mode before they can communicate with Windows. Check your camera documentation to confirm this if you are unsure.*

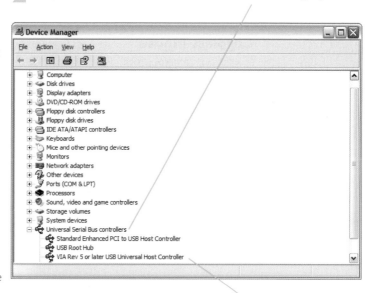

*XP's USB drivers are supported as standard system drivers, but may not be compatible with the digicam's software. You may need to download an update to the software from the manufacturer's website.*

3 Right-click USB Universal Host Controller and click Uninstall.

Reboot the computer and on restart XP will automatically reinstall the USB driver. Reconnect the camera and you should now be able to download your snaps.

# Mouse Troubleshooting

*If the mouse is working, but in an erratic or jerky fashion, it needs cleaning.*

Turn the mouse over and remove the rubber ball – give it a good clean. Then have a look inside the mouse itself, where you will see some little plastic rollers (usually three). In the middle of each, you will see a line of dirt running right round the circumference. This is the cause of the problem: the dirt is preventing the ball from making a smooth contact with the rollers, resulting in jerky movement of the cursor. Clean the dirt off, and the mouse will be as good as new. The problem can also be caused by the surface you are using the mouse on: mice don't work well on smooth shiny surfaces.

If your mouse's buttons aren't functioning properly, they also could need cleaning. Take the mouse apart and spray contact cleaner onto the contacts and switches inside the mouse, depressing the buttons several times to work the cleaner in.

*In practice, optical mice do not have the issues with debris build-up that mechanical ball mice do. However, if you experience some erratic mouse behavior, check that the light-emitting diode on the underside of the device isn't being obstructed in some way.*

## Standard Mouse

Obvious things first – check the mouse is not connected to the wrong port. At the top rear of the system case you will see the keyboard and mouse ports, which are identical. It's an easy mistake to make. If it's a USB mouse, check its USB connection. Try connecting to a different USB port. Check that USB is enabled in the BIOS.

Next, make sure the mouse is installed. Check this out in the Device Manager under "Mice and other pointing devices." Then try restarting the computer in Safe Mode; if the mouse now works then the mouse driver may be conflicting with another device. Again, check this out in the Device Manager.

If Device Manager reports no problems, then the driver may be corrupt. Uninstall it by right-clicking and selecting Uninstall. Reboot the PC and XP will reinstall it. If the mouse doesn't work in Safe Mode either, and the connections are sound, then the mouse is faulty: replace it.

## Cordless Mouse

If you are using a cordless mouse, carry out all of the above checks. If it still doesn't work, replace the batteries (you will usually experience a general slowing down of mouse operation before the batteries die completely, though).

Check that the mouse hasn't lost its connection with the receiver, by holding the mouse next to it and clicking a button.

Verify that the mouse and the receiver are operating at the same frequency, by removing the batteries from the mouse and then replacing them. This will reset both the mouse and the receiver to the same frequency.

Check that the mouse is no more than two yards from the receiver, and remove any possible source of RF interference, such as a cordless phone or other transmitting device, from the area.

If there is still no joy, connect the mouse to another computer. If it doesn't work there either, then replace it.

# Games/Multimedia Troubleshooting

Gaming is one of the most common applications to which a personal computer is put. This chapter investigates typical problems that users experience when playing their games, and also offers some handy tips to enhance this popular pastime.

Multimedia has been a somewhat neglected aspect of Windows in the past, but with the latest Media Player this is no longer the case. The extensive development put into this application clearly demonstrates Microsoft's intention to eventually build complete home entertainment systems around the PC.

However, tightly integrated as it is with Internet Explorer and system components such as DirectX, Media Player is inevitably prone to problems and errors.

## Covers

Chapter Eleven

# Games Don't Run With XP

Another way to access the Program Accessibility utility is to right-click the game's Setup or Install file. You will then see a dialog box with a Compatibility tab, which will offer the same options as the wizard.

NOTE: If you do this from the games CD, any settings will be lost when you close the game. The next time you run the game, you'll have to set it up again. However, if you copy the game files to the hard disk and apply the compatibility settings from there, then the settings will be permanently retained.

The Program Compatibility utility can also be used for other software applications that worked with previous versions of Windows but not XP. The procedure is exactly the same.

Many games require the computer system to have 3D video capabilities before they will work. Usually this will require a dedicated video adapter, although more recent systems may also have 3D-capable video built in to the mainboard.

If your games won't play, and you don't have a separate video adapter, check that your onboard video is 3D-compatible.

This is a very common problem, and is due to the fact that XP's underlying architecture is fundamentally different to earlier versions of Windows home operating systems. Many games that played fine on ME and earlier just won't run on XP.

In an effort to overcome this problem, Microsoft have included a Program Compatibility utility with XP, which will in many cases get your games running. This works by re-creating the operating system environment that these games were designed for.

Give the Program Compatibility utility a try as follows:

1 Insert your game CD and then go to Start, All Programs, Accessories, Compatibility Wizard.

![Help and Support Center window showing the Program Compatibility Wizard with options: "I want to choose from a list of programs", "I want to use the program in the CD-ROM drive" (selected), "I want to locate the program manually".]

2 At the first screen click Next. At the second screen click "I want to use the program in the CD-ROM drive" and click Next.

3 In the next screen you will see options for: 256 colors, 640 x 480 Screen Resolution and Disable Visual Themes. Select any that may be applicable and then click Next and Next again in the final screen.

If the game still won't run, try selecting different options in step 3.

# Games Don't Play Properly

*Outdated sound card drivers can also cause problems when playing games. Download updates from the manufacturer's website.*

Your game play is slow, jerky, intermittent, or crashes or freezes your PC. Graphics are blocky. The screen goes black. If you experience any of these things when playing a game, check the following:

## System Resources

Of all the applications that can be run on a PC, games are the most demanding in terms of system resources – RAM and CPU processing power in particular. If your system is not up to scratch in this respect, you will have problems. Check the game's recommended system requirements, which will be listed on the box and in the documentation. Then see if your system is up to the required specifications; if not, you may have to upgrade it. Before you do, though, try a few simple steps that can sometimes free up enough resources to just make the difference:

*You can find out your system's specifications in the Control Panel by clicking System. Your RAM and CPU details will be on the General tab. Alternatively, you can go to Start, All Programs, Accessories, System Tools and System Information. System Information will give you much more detail about your system's specifications.*

- Switch off and then restart the PC. This will clear the memory.

- Make sure no other applications are running.

- Lower your screen resolution (as described on page 83) and your display refresh rate (as described on page 82).

Finally, try setting up XP for best performance (as opposed to best appearance) as described below:

*Closing a running application doesn't necessarily mean it will release the memory it was using. Sometimes programs will leave fragments of themselves behind. The only way to completely clear RAM is to switch off the PC, as it will only retain data as long as it is powered up.*

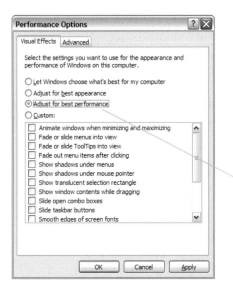

1 Go to Start, Control Panel, System, Advanced, Performance, Settings, Visual Effects.

2 Tick "Adjust for best performance."

*DirectX is a set of Application Program Interfaces (APIs) developed by Microsoft that enable programmers to write programs that access hardware features of a computer without knowing exactly what hardware will be installed on the machine. DirectX achieves this by creating an intermediate layer that translates generic hardware commands into specific commands for particular items of hardware. In particular, DirectX lets multimedia applications take advantage of hardware acceleration features supported by video accelerators.*

*If the checks opposite indicate any problems with DirectX, then reinstall it. While you're at it, install the latest version. Even if your game does not need the latest version, the system as a whole will benefit. You can get DirectX from the Microsoft website or from the cover CD of computer magazines.*

## Video Adapter

Outdated video adapter drivers can have an adverse effect on games, recent ones in particular. Visit the manufacturer's website and download the latest drivers for your model.

## DirectX

DirectX is a technology developed by Microsoft that facilitates the displaying of multimedia elements, such as full color graphics, video, and 3D animation. The majority of modern games are written around this technology and require a specific version of DirectX to be installed on the computer. Check it out as follows:

1 Go to Start, Run. In the Run box type Dxdiag then click OK. In the DirectX Diagnostic Tool, click the System tab.

2 Installed version of DirectX.

3 Click the DirectX Files tab and, under Notes, check that there are no reported problems.

*DirectDraw is a software interface standard for transferring video processing from a PC's CPU to the video adapter. When the CPU is not busy, the Windows Graphics Display Interface (GDI) updates the video display. If the CPU is busy, DirectDraw allows an application to send update information directly to the video adapter. DirectDraw can also provide applications, such as games, direct access to features of particular display devices.*

*Direct3D is an application program interface for manipulating and displaying three-dimensional objects. Developed by Microsoft, Direct3D provides programmers with a way to develop 3D programs that can utilize whatever video adapter is installed in the machine. Virtually all 3D video adapters support Direct3D.*

*Try reducing your OpenGL and Direct3D Performance Settings, which may be set higher than your system can support. Do this as follows:
Right-click the Desktop, select Properties and click the Settings tab. Click Advanced and you will see the OpenGL and Direct3D tabs. Click these in turn and drag the slider to the best performance position.*

## Hardware Acceleration

Try lowering your hardware acceleration. Do the following:

Right-click the Desktop and select Properties. Click the Settings tab and click Advanced.

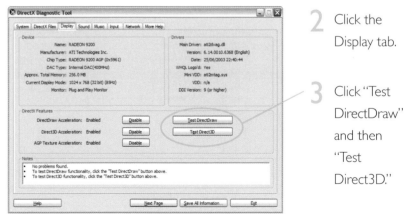

2 Click the Troubleshoot tab and drag the slider to the None position. Reboot, and run the game again. If the original problem has cleared, increase the hardware acceleration and try again. Do this until you achieve the highest setting that will allow the game to play.

## DirectDraw & Direct3D

Check that your system supports these as follows:

Go to Start, Run. In the Run box type Dxdiag, then Click OK.

2 Click the Display tab.

3 Click "Test DirectDraw" and then "Test Direct3D."

# Useful Games Tips

*Most game installation routines give you an option to do a minimal install, which basically means that most of the game files are left on the CD. This option can be useful if hard disk space is an issue. However, if it isn't, use the full installation option. This will enable the game to access its files from the hard disk, which results in smoother game play.*

*Virtual CD-ROM programs can create up to 23 virtual CD drives on your machine. This means you can have up to 23 different games preloaded and ready to go. You can put the CDs in a drawer and then forget about them.*

*Also, as the games are being played from the hard disk, they will perform better. Another advantage of these programs is that they can override most manufacturers' copy protection methods.*

One of the most irritating things about playing games on a PC is the constant need to be inserting and swapping CDs. Apart from the nuisance, a frequently used CD might eventually become scratched enough to prevent it playing properly – see page 61.

Many people try copying the CD to the hard disk and then installing the game from there. This will work, but only up to the point where you try to play the game – then you will get a "No disk in CD drive" error message. This is manufacturer's copy protection at work.

There is, however, a simple way to eliminate CD swapping:

## Virtual CD-ROM Drives

A virtual CD-ROM drive is an emulated drive created by a software program. The software creates an image of the game CD on the hard disk, which can then be played in the virtual drive without the CD. A good example of this type of program is CDSpace, available from www.cdspace.com.

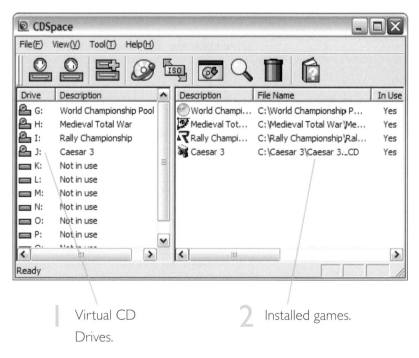

1 Virtual CD Drives.

2 Installed games.

*Games sites such as gamecopyworld also offer reviews of all the latest games, training manuals, game demos and much more. Any serious gamer will find these sites a mine of information and useful downloads.*

## Cheats & Add-ons

Many sites, games sites in particular, have "Cheats" available for free download. These do just what the name implies – allow you to cheat by overcoming obstacles in the game that are preventing you from progressing to further levels, for example.

You can also obtain add-ons for specific games from these sites, such as extra aircraft for flight simulators (you might have to pay for these though).

## Game Controllers

To get the best out of your games you will definitely need a dedicated high-quality controller. The cheapo affair that was supplied with your PC will not cut the mustard. Throw it away and invest in a proper model.

*Another advantage of a high-quality controller is that the software allows you to create profiles. Simply set up your game, i.e. program the buttons according to your requirements, and then create a profile for that game. The next time you run it, select the appropriate profile and the buttons are automatically configured.*

What type you get depends on the games you play. Flight sims work best with a yoke, while driving games will benefit from a dedicated steering wheel and brake pedal. However, if this type of setup is likely to damage your street cred, a driving game will also work well with a joystick.

Gamepads are good all-round controllers and will usually have a HAT control plus several programmable buttons and sometimes a mini joystick as well. An example from Saitek is shown below.

1 Hat control.  2 Programmable buttons.

# Media Player Won't Play Movies

*If the video file is on a DVD, there are a number of other things that can prevent it from playing. These issues are discussed on pages 62–64.*

*When WMP encounters a file for which it cannot find a suitable codec, it searches a Microsoft site that holds a database of various codecs. If the required codec is in this database, it is automatically downloaded and installed. It is also possible for a user to access this site and manually download these codecs. If you wish to do this go to: www.microsoft.com/windows/ windowsmedia/format/ codecdownload.aspx.*

*If you have a video file that won't play, and you don't know the required codec, you need a codec detection program. One such utility is the compellingly named "Gspot" available from www.headbands.com/gspot. This application will tell you the specific codec needed for both video and sound.*

## Missing Codecs

One of the most common problems is when a video file is opened but Windows Media Player (WMP) just plays a visualization (as shown below).

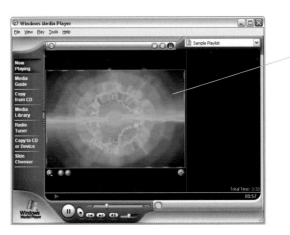

Visualizations are very pretty but you'd rather see your movie.

When this happens it means that WMP hasn't been able to find the correct codec. Codecs are small pieces of software that are used to compress a video or sound file when it is created, in order to reduce the file size. When the file is played it is decompressed; to do that, the codec that created it must be on the computer.

The most used type of video codec is AVI, of which there are several versions. The two most common are DIVX and XVID. If you get the above problem, you need to download and install both of these, as it's almost certain the file will have been compressed with one or the other. You can find them at www.divxmovies.com.

## Corrupted File

It's not uncommon for a video file to be corrupted in some way. If it's been downloaded from the Internet, the corruption could have happened during the download; if it's on a CD or DVD, the disc could be damaged. Try playing the video in a different player such as Media Player 2 (type mplayer2 in the Start menu Run box). If it still won't open then you know it's corrupt. There are various video file repair utilities available on the Internet with which you could try and repair the file. Failing this, obtain another copy or download it again.

# Media Player Playback Problems

*Windows Media Player is tightly integrated with several operating system components, DirectX in particular. Therefore, any problems with DirectX can have serious knock-on effects with WMP.*

*To find out exactly which codecs are installed on your system, go to Start, Control Panel, System, Hardware and Device Manager. From the View menu, click Devices by connection. In the new dialog box, scroll down until you see Video Codecs. Right-click this and select Properties. In the next dialog box click the Properties tab.*

*While you have this window open, check to see that you don't have multiple versions of the same codec installed, which can also cause problems. If you have, delete all but one of them.*

*Many codec packs are untested compilations of various codecs and filters commonly used on the Internet. These are known to cause problems with WMP.*

## Movie Playback is Poor

Your movies are jerky, they flicker or you see lines on the screen.

The above issues are often a result of an under-powered system. In this case, you will find that WMP takes a long time to load as well. The only solutions are to make more resources available to WMP or to upgrade your PC's RAM and CPU.

The next thing is to check that DirectX is correctly installed, as described on page 122. Also, upgrade to the latest version. The same applies to your video adapter. A lot of problems are caused by outdated or incompatible video drivers.

Your video acceleration rate may be too high. Reduce it as follows:

1 From the Tools menu in WMP, select Options. Click the Performance tab.

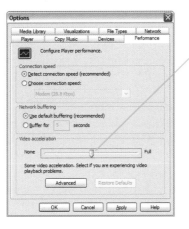

2 Drag the Video Acceleration slider back. Experiment with this until you reach the best setting.

If your movie playback is still poor then you probably have a problem with the codecs installed on your system, particularly if WMP is prone to crashing as well.

This particular issue is often caused by the various codec packs available for download from the Internet. Incompatibilities are known to exist between some of the components in these packs, which can cause serious playback issues in WMP. If you have any of these packs on your system, uninstall them.

# Media Player & The Internet

*Streaming is a technique for transferring data in such a way that it can be processed as a steady and continuous stream. Streaming technologies are becoming increasingly important with the growth of the Internet because most users do not have fast enough access to download large multimedia files quickly. With streaming, the client browser or plug-in can start displaying the data before the entire file has been downloaded.*

WMP comes with improved media streaming capabilities. This process was developed due to the often huge size of Internet multimedia files and the slow download times offered by a telephone line connection. Streaming allows the media to be watched or listened to as the download is taking place.

## Media File Doesn't Play

You click on a media link but WMP won't play it. There are several causes of this:

It could be those pesky codecs again. If WMP can't find the necessary codec on your system or in its download database, it won't play the file. Alternatively, the file could be corrupt.

Your computer may be behind a firewall that has not had the appropriate ports opened for use with Netshow Services. The solution is to open the necessary ports.

*Netshow Services is one of the streaming media components of WMP, and enables the streaming of audio and video over the Internet. A protocol is a standard for the transmission of data over a network. There are various types, each with its pros and cons (such as reliability and speed).*

The media file may be using a protocol that WMP is not configured to use. On WMP's Tools menu, click Options, and then click the Network tab. In the Streaming Protocols area, select all the protocol checkboxes. Try playing the file again. If it still won't play then WMP does not support the protocol.

While this window is open, also check your proxy server settings. If you do not know what these should be, select a protocol, click Configure, and then select Autodetect Proxy Settings.

## Playback Quality is Poor

Playback stops periodically. This problem is caused by network congestion, which is preventing WMP's buffer from being replenished quickly enough.

*Some sites require cookies to be enabled in your browser, so disabling cookies may disable WMP's ability to play a file – see page 149.*

About the only thing you can do here is to increase the size of the buffer. Do this by selecting Options from WMP's Tools menu and clicking the Performance tab. Tick Buffer For and in the box enter a higher setting (60 is the maximum).

If that doesn't work, then you'll just have to try later when hopefully the network is less congested.

# Media Player & CD/DVD Burning

Windows Media Player comes with CD/DVD mastering facilities, which allows the user to rip audio and video discs. It is also possible to create data discs with WMP.

Problems likely to be encountered when disk mastering with WMP include the following:

## WMP Won't Burn All the Audio Files

This is a common problem with WMP. Basically what happens is that it will burn a few files and then stop with an error message to the effect that it cannot fit the rest of the files onto the disc. This is misleading – the problem is actually that the burn process has been interrupted for some reason and WMP has automatically closed or finalized the disc, which means no more data can be burned to it. See page 72 for more details on disc closing.

If you get this problem, reboot the PC to clear the system's memory and make sure no other applications are running. If it happens again, then use a dedicated disk mastering program.

## WMP Won't Burn or Copy MP3 Files

WMP does not support MP3 file copying/burning. It will play them, but to copy/burn them you need to install a third-party MP3 decoder.

## WMP Doesn't Burn Any Files

Your digital/analog settings are not compatible, i.e. WMP is set to digital and your CD/DVD drive is set to analog, or vice versa.

WMP has two ways of burning:
Digital – which is enabled by default as most PC and Internet media is digital.
Analog – which has to be selected and typically is used when burning tracks from video cassettes, tape and vinyl records.

To select which method you want, you need to alter settings in both WMP and Device Manager. To make the change in WMP go to the Tools menu and select Options. Click the Devices tab, click your disk drive, click Properties and then in the Playback area on the Audio tab, click Digital. In Device Manager, right-click the disk drive, click Properties and then click the Properties tab. Tick the box for digital, untick it for analog.

# Miscellaneous Media Player Faults

*Poor quality sound in WMP can usually be fixed by updating the driver for your sound card and ensuring the latest version of DirectX is installed.*

*Also, reducing your audio Hardware Acceleration can often effect a cure. Do this by going to Start, Control Panel, Sounds and Audio Devices. Click the Audio tab, Advanced and then Performance.*

*Windows Media Rights Management is a secure technology that helps protect the rights of content owners, while enabling consumers to obtain digital content easily and legitimately. Windows Media Rights Management "locks" digital media files with a license key to maintain content protection, even if these files are widely distributed. Each license is uniquely assigned to a computer; this prevents illegal distribution of digital media files.*

*If WMP disconnects sometimes when it starts playing Internet media content, it may be detecting your connection speed incorrectly. You can manually specify your connection speed on the Performance tab of the Options dialog box.*

## Audio Crackles And/Or Skips During Playback.

Try enabling Error Correction in WMP. From the Tools menu, select Options and then click the Devices tab. Click Properties and click Use Error Correction.

If that doesn't help, switch to using analog playback as described on page 129.

If you're getting background noise from your speakers, mute the Line In and Microphone input in your system's volume settings.

## Burned Discs will Play On Only My PC

You've burned a disc to give to a friend, but it won't play on your friend's PC. However, it will play fine on yours.

This is WMP's Digital Rights Management at work, which is intended to protect you against having your media files copied. This is very thoughtful of WMP, but what if you don't need your files protecting? The easy solution is to disable this feature by going to Tools, Options, Copy Music and removing the check mark from the Protect Content box.

## Radio Station Favorites Keep Disappearing

Radio Station favorites are stored as Internet Explorer cookies. If you are in the habit of periodically clearing your cookie cache, the radio station favorites will be cleared as well.

## WMP Won't Support Digital Playback on the CD-ROM drive

Firstly, check that digital playback is enabled for the drive in Device Manager, as described on page 129.

Secondly, WMP tests the quality of the digital signal. If the CD-ROM is giving a "dirty" read, WMP will reject digital playback on that drive, as this can give rise to serious errors. This is common with older CD drives and the solution is to buy a new one.

## WMP Won't Switch to Full Screen

Check that Hardware Acceleration is set to full (see page 123).

Install the latest version of DirectX.

Update your video adapter driver.

# Modem Troubleshooting

The two types of modem used with computers are dial-up and cable.

Most modem problems are associated with the dial-up type, although very often the perceived problem is actually a fault on the network that the modem is connected to or trying to connect to.

Cable modems are used with broadband connections and are always "on." This, coupled with the fact that cable connections are much faster than dial-up, eliminates many of the issues that dial-up users have to contend with.

This chapter investigates issues that prevent modems from establishing a connection.

## Covers

**Chapter Twelve**

# Dial-up Modem Doesn't Dial

Regardless of whether your modem is operational or not, there are two things that must be in place before it will dial out:

## Working Telephone Connection

This is straightforward enough to establish. Remove the modem cable from the phone socket and plug in a telephone. If you hear a dial tone, then you have a connection.

## Does Windows Know the Modem is There?

The second thing is, does XP know your modem is in the system? It may be plugged in to the mainboard and be perfectly functional, but has XP "seen" it? Find out as follows:

1. Go to Start, Control Panel, System, Hardware, Device Manager.

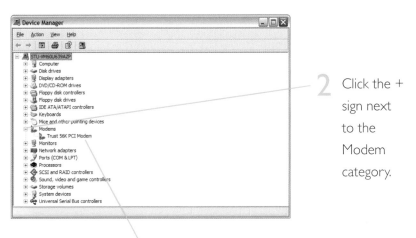

2. Click the + sign next to the Modem category.

3. Name and model of the installed modem.

If the modem is showing in Device Manager, as shown above, go to the next page.

However, if there is no modem category at all, then it hasn't been installed. Put the modem driver CD in the CD drive, reboot and on restart XP should now recognize the device and automatically start the Add Hardware wizard to install the driver. The modem will then show up in the Device Manager. If it still won't work though, go to the next page.

*If you see two or more modems listed in the modem category, this can be as bad as seeing none. Having several drivers installed for the same device is almost guaranteed to cause problems. This is because the drivers will be competing for the same system files and IRQs thus preventing each other from working. In this case, establish which is the correct driver and uninstall the others.*

If your modem is showing up in the Device Manager but isn't working then the problem could be a corrupted or incorrect driver. In this situation you may see a warning symbol next to the device. If so, right-click the device and select Properties to reveal the problem. Otherwise, do the following:

1   In the Device Manager, highlight the modem and from the right-click menu, click Uninstall.

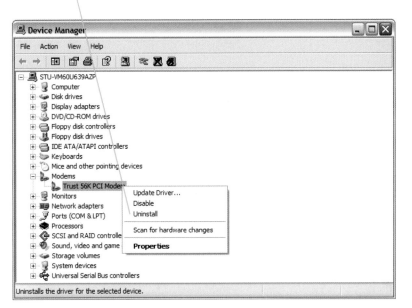

*A common connection problem is when a user receives an error message saying "The Modem is Busy or Not Responding." The usual cause of this is that the modem is already running because it wasn't disconnected at the end of the previous session.*

2   You will now see a message warning that you are about to uninstall this device from your system. Click OK.

Reboot the computer and, on restart, XP will recognize the modem. This will be indicated by a yellow pop-up message just above the system tray.

XP will now automatically reinstall the modem driver. Try the modem again, and if it still won't work go to the next page.

# Dial-up Modem Diagnostic Test

*The computer communicates with the modem using a command set, often referred to as the AT Command Set. These commands are used to configure, diagnose and receive information from the modem.*

*Modem commands can either be used as part of an initialization string in a specific program, or can be issued directly to the modem by the user.*

*As an example of this, you can silence the modem when it's dialing by doing the following: Go to the Device Manager, right-click the modem, select Properties and click the Advanced tab. In the Extra Initialization Commands box enter ATM0. From now on you won't hear the strangulated buzzes, clicks and whirrs as the modem connects.*

*XP comes with another utility that can be useful in troubleshooting modem and network problems: the Network Diagnostic utility, which can be found in System Information. Access this by going to Start, All Programs, Accessories and System Tools. Click System Information and from the Tools menu click Net Diagnostics.*

*Net Diagnostics runs a check on your modem and network adapters, giving a status check plus a list of all the settings currently assigned to the relevant devices.*

Having established that the modem is correctly installed, the next thing is to find out if it's working.

Do this as follows:

1 Open the Device Manager in the Control Panel, locate the modem entry and right-click it. Select Properties. In the dialog box that opens, click the Diagnostics tab.

2 Click Query Modem.

3 If you now see a list of AT commands, this indicates that the modem is working and that the problem is software-related.

If the list of AT commands appears as shown in the above screenshot, then go to page 136.

If the commands don't appear or you see a "Port Already In Use" message, then the modem has failed the diagnostic test. This indicates that it is incorrectly configured: Go to the next page.

# Dial-up Modem Configuration

*Analog telephone lines were not designed for Internet access. They are, in fact, totally unsuitable for this type of use, as the bandwidth (data transfer capacities) they offer simply isn't enough to adequately cope with the ever-increasing volume of traffic the Internet generates. The strength and reliability of connection they provide is also weak and thus easily broken.*

## Modem COM Port

The first thing to check is that your modem is configured to use the correct COM port. Consult the modem documentation to establish which port your modem is designed to operate from. Then do the following:

1. In Device Manager, right-click the modem and select Properties. Click the Advanced tab and then Advanced Port Settings.

2. Check that the modem is set to the port given in the documentation.

3. If it is set to the wrong port, select the correct one by using the drop-down box (next to COM Port Number). Click OK.

*If the Advanced Port Settings option is not displayed, the modem does not support changing the assigned COM port. In this situation, you must reinstall the modem and choose the desired COM port during the installation.*

## COM Port Settings

Now we need to make sure the port's settings are correct. First make sure that the port settings are not conflicting with another device. Check this out in the Device Manager.

Then check the modem's connection speed is correctly set.

*If your data transfer rate is set too high, your modem may not be able to connect to a modem that has a lower data transfer rate, or you may experience problems with your communications program. To determine whether this is the problem, reset the data transfer rate by lowering your port speed.*

1. Open the modem's Properties dialog box by right-clicking the modem and clicking Properties.

2. Click the Modem tab and set the Maximum Port Speed to that of your modem. This will be in the documentation; usually it will be 57600.

# Dial-up Modem Software

*As a last ditch attempt, you can try installing one of XP's generic modem drivers. These are "no frills" drivers, which will work with any modem. Do the following:*

*1) In Device Manager, right-click the Modem and click Uninstall. Then run the Add Hardware wizard from the Control Panel.*

*2) At the first screen, click Next.*

*3) In the second, tick "Yes, I have already connected the hardware."*

*4) In the third, scroll down to the bottom and click "Add a new hardware device."*

*5) In the fourth, tick "Install the hardware that I manually select from a list (advanced)."*

*6) In the fifth, click Modems.*

*7) In the sixth, click "Don't detect my modem, I will select it from a list."*

*8) In the seventh, select Standard 56000 bps modem.*

*9) In the final screen, highlight the COM port and then click Next.*

*XP will now install a Standard 56000 bps modem driver. Assuming your modem is not faulty it should now work, although it won't perform optimally.*

*If the above procedure does the trick, it indicates that the first driver was almost certainly the incorrect version for the modem.*

*Before you throw the modem in the trash can, open up the system case and make sure it is firmly connected to the mainboard.*

The modem is now correctly installed and configured. If it is still refusing to dial out, the next thing to check is the communication software it is using, in case this has been corrupted. The easiest way to do this is to uninstall and then reinstall it.

1 Go to the Control Panel and open Network Connections.

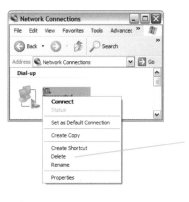

2 Right-click the dial-up connection and click Properties. Make a note of all of the settings on the various tabs, and then click OK.

3 Right-click the connection and click Delete.

Now you need to reinstall your connection. If this was originally created with a CD from your ISP, insert the disc and follow the instructions.

Alternatively, you can use XP's New Connection wizard.

1 From the File menu of Network Connections, click New Connection.

2 Reinstall your connection with the New Connection wizard using the settings you noted earlier.

If the modem now dials out, then the communications program was corrupted. If it still doesn't work, then the modem is almost certainly faulty.

# Cable Modem Connection Issues

## Internet Connection

Most cable modem Internet connections are via CATV networks, which were originally designed and used for cable TV distribution.

It wasn't long though, before the cable companies saw the potential of their networks for Internet access due to their spare bandwidth. All they needed to do was add an upload channel.

If you find yourself unable to connect to the Internet or to send or receive emails, before you do anything else make sure you have a live Internet connection. Do this as follows:

1 Go to the Control Panel and open Network Connections.

3 Your connection status is shown here.

2 Click your connection and you will see the dialog box below.

Given the high access speeds it offers, plus the fact that the connection is always on, broadband is much more user-friendly than analog telephone connections.

If step 3 shows your connection to be "Connected," it doesn't necessarily mean, however, that the network itself is OK. It could well be down for technical reasons – it does happen occasionally. You can check this in two ways. If your TV runs off the same cable network, see if it is receiving a signal. Alternatively, phone the service provider. Often, they will provide a taped message advising of any current technical problems.

## Modem Connections

Some ISP software will include a diagnostic utility that can be used to check the validity of a connection and also whether or not the modem is actually receiving data from the network. Check out your installation disc.

The next thing to check is that the PC is connected to the modem. Cable modems come with two types of connection – USB and Ethernet.

USB modems will connect directly to a USB port on the PC, while Ethernet modems will connect to an Ethernet adapter. These can be external or internal devices.

Using the cable modem screenshot opposite as an example, the various LEDs indicate:

**PWR** – lit when the modem is powered up.
**USB** – lit when there is a physical USB connection to the PC. Flashes when transferring data.
**ENET** – same as USB, but for Ethernet.
**U/S** – normally unlit. Flashes when transmitting data to the cable network.
**D/S** – normally unlit. Flashes when receiving data from the cable network.
**SYNC** – lit when the modem is locked on to the downstream signal.
**RDY** – lit when the cable modem is ready for use.

NOTE: The exact labels for these lights will vary between manufacturers. However, the lights on all cable modems will indicate similar information.

Don't forget the possibility that a third-party device such as a router, hub or signal splitter is faulty. If you have one of these on the system, disconnect it and connect the modem directly to the cable input.

To check that your connection is working (in other words that the PC is communicating with the modem) take a look at the front panel of the modem. Here you will see a row of LED lights. Two of these, USB and ENET, indicate whether or not the respective connection is working.

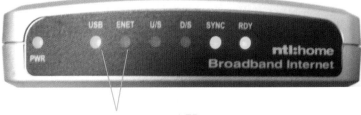

USB and Ethernet connection LEDs.

If the LED indicates a problem with a USB connection, check that the cable is securely connected at both ends. If you are using a new or upgraded PC for the first time, USB may be not be enabled on the system. Check this out as described on page 117. If USB is enabled, the problem could be caused by a corrupt driver; reinstall it.

If the problem is with an Ethernet connection, again, the first thing to check is the Ethernet cable's connections. Then go into the Device Manager and check that the Ethernet adapter is installed and doesn't have any reported problems. If in any doubt, simply uninstall it by right-clicking and selecting Uninstall. Then reboot and Windows will automatically reinstall the driver.

## Third-Party Devices

If your modem cable passes through a router, then disconnect the router and connect the cable direct to the PC.

Similarly, if you are using a signal splitter so that you can connect the cable to another device such as a TV, remove the splitter so that the modem is connected directly to the cable input.

# Cable Modem Software Issues

Having established that the network is OK and that the modem is communicating with the PC, the problem is either software-related or a fault with the modem itself. Of the two, a software issue is far more likely. Check it out as follows:

## Reset the Modem

Many computer problems can be fixed by simply switching off for a few seconds and then restarting; this applies equally to cable modems. This is the first thing to try. Some cable modems will have a reset button on the front panel for this purpose.

However, switching off the PC, disconnecting the modem and then reconnecting it before switching the PC back on again, is a better approach to take. Doing it this way can address a range of hardware and software issues.

NOTE: cable modems have to go through an initialization sequence before they are ready to go. This can take several minutes and is indicated by the LEDs flashing.

## Firewalls

Some people swear by these utilities, others swear at them. Loathe them or love them, however, it is a fact that they are essential if you have an "always on" broadband connection.

Unfortunately, firewalls can and do cause network problems. In worst case scenarios they can block Internet access completely. If you are having connection problems, try disabling any firewall you may have active and see if this resolves the issue. If it does you need to check its settings.

When resetting your cable modem, it's important that you do it the correct way.

Although pressing the reset button (if there is one) will resolve some issues, there are others that it won't.

Carry out the procedure as follows:

1) Switch off the PC.

2) Disconnect the modem.

3) Reconnect the modem and allow it to initialize (wait for the lights to stop blinking).

4) Switch the PC back on.

Internet Connection Sharing is a Windows application that has been around since Windows 98 SE. It allows two or more networked computers to share a single Internet connection, whether it is DSL, ISDN, cable, T1, satellite or dial-up.

While XP's version of ICS is an improvement over previous versions, there are still many issues with it that can cause disruption to a network connection. If you are having connection problems and have ICS set up, uninstall it and see if that effects a cure.

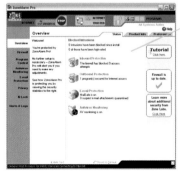

Zone Alarm firewall.

Before you activate your firewall, make sure it is configured correctly. Otherwise you may have all sorts of network problems.

*Two or more instances of a network connection will very likely result in neither of them working. Open Network Connections in the Control Panel and make sure there is only one Local Area Connection.*

*Similarly, make sure there is only one cable modem installed. Check this in Device Manager under the Network Adapters category. Uninstall any duplicated entries.*

*What exactly does the Network Connection Repair tool do? Given the split second it takes to run, seemingly not a lot. Well, actually it does quite a lot, including the following:*

*1) The Dynamic Host Configuration Protocol (DHCP) lease is renewed.*

*2) The Address Resolution Protocol (ARP) cache is flushed.*

*3) The NetBIOS name cache is reloaded.*

*4) The NetBIOS name update is sent.*

*5) The Domain Name System (DNS) cache is flushed.*

*6) DNS name registration.*

*7) IEEE 802.1X Authentication Restart (SP1 or later).*

*Problems with any of the above will cause connection problems.*

*Don't forget XP's System Restore. If you are really stuck, it might be worth giving this a try, as described on page 38.*

## MAC Addresses

A MAC address is a unique identifying number assigned to all network devices.

Most domestic ISPs have their cable modems configured to recognize only one client PC. This is achieved by the MAC address of the PC's network interface. Once the modem has learned the MAC address of a PC, it will not respond to a different MAC address (that is, to a different PC).

So, if you've connected the modem to a new or upgraded PC and find that you cannot get an Internet connection, this is the reason. Fortunately, it is a simple matter to resolve. All you have to do is reset the cable modem by powering it off and then on again. Once the modem has rebooted and synchronized itself (LEDs stopped flashing), reboot the PC.

## Repair the Connection

XP provides a useful connection repair utility. Open Network Connections in the Control Panel.

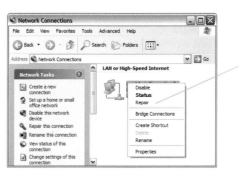

Right-click the connection and click Repair.

## Reinstall the Connection

If all else fails, then the connection itself is probably corrupt. Repair it by reinstalling the software. If you set up your connection using a CD from your ISP, then use this and follow the instructions. Alternatively, you can do it with the New Connection wizard. Open Network Connections and from the File menu, click New Connection. Follow the steps in the wizard.

If, after all this, you still cannot establish a connection, consider replacing your cable modem.

# Internet/Email Troubleshooting

This chapter investigates common problems that users experience when using the Internet. These range from inability to access specific sites to broken and intermittent connections. As most of these issues are specific to dial-up connections, this is the medium we will be referring to unless otherwise stated.

Email is, without a doubt, the most popular of all the Internet applications. Most problems here, however, relate to the email application itself, rather than the Internet network. We shall see how to correctly check and configure email software and also how to resolve common problems.

## Covers

Chapter Thirteen

# Intermittent Connections

*Idle disconnect is a safety feature that automatically disconnects the modem after a specified period. Its purpose is to prevent a user from clocking up a huge telephone bill if, for some reason, he or she forgets to log off.*

Troubleshooting in this chapter assumes that you already have a working connection to the Internet. If you don't, or are in doubt, refer to the Modem Troubleshooting chapter.

You lose your connection at periodic intervals for no apparent reason. There are several causes of this problem.

## Idle Disconnect

If your connection keeps failing after exactly the same period, do the following:

*A bad Internet connection might actually have nothing to do with your setup, but rather the ISP's. If the connection is consistently poor, simply try a different ISP. There's nothing to stop you having two or more separate accounts. If you are having problems with one then just switch to the other.*

*Also, bear in mind that ISPs who offer the lowest rates will probably also offer the lowest quality of service.*

Go to Start, Control Panel, Phone and Modem Options. Click the Modems tab, highlight and right-click your modem. From the right-click menu, click Properties. In the next dialog box click Options.

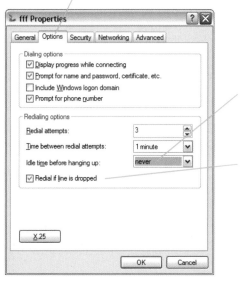

2 Set "Idle time before hanging up" to Never.

3 You may as well tick the "Redial if line is dropped" box as well. This will save you having to manually redial in future.

*Ensure that all memory phones and faxes are disconnected from the line. Some of these have small rechargeable capacitors that maintain the memory of the device; these capacitors recharge from the phone line approximately every 15 minutes, and in some cases can disconnect the modem.*

## Programs/Devices that Activate Suddenly

Applications such as Advanced Power Management and screensavers can break your connection when they "kick in." Try disabling them.

Remove any other devices connected to the telephone line that might be causing interference, such as phones, answering machines and fax machines. These can all cause a connection to be dropped.

## Call Waiting

If this feature is enabled, it can break your Internet connection when another call comes in. Disable it as follows:

*Call waiting is a method of alerting someone who's using a phone that someone else is trying to ring them. This is indicated by a beep. If the phone line is being used for Internet access, this beep can break the connection and, even if it doesn't, will cause the connection to pause or slow down for a short period. You can eliminate this by disabling call waiting as described opposite. However, then you won't know when someone is trying to contact you.*

*If you need to know this, there are several options available:*

*1) You can buy a call waiting modem, which lets you know if there's an incoming call and provides answering options.*

*2) Get a second phone line.*

*3) Upgrade your connection to Broadband.*

*4) Try an Internet Call Waiting Service.*

1 Open Phone and Modem Options in the Control Panel. Highlight the connection and then click Edit.

2 Tick "To disable call waiting dial:". In the box, select *70.

## Transmit/Receive Buffers

The COM port transmit/receive buffers are used to regulate the flow of data between the modem and PC. If they are set too high, connection problems can result. Try resetting them as follows:

1 Go to Control Panel, Phone & Modem Options. Click the modem, and click Properties. Then click the Advanced tab and Advanced Port Settings (see bottom margin note).

*The Advanced Port Settings dialog box may not be available with certain modems.*

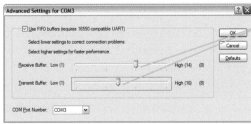

2 Lower the size of the buffers by dragging the sliders to the left.

The best setting will be a trade-off between speed and performance.

*Download managers can also be configured to begin a download at a specified time. They will automatically open the Internet connection using the user's dial-up network settings, connect to the website and then begin the download. If the connection fails during the download for any reason, they will redial and then resume the download. When the download is complete they will close the connection.*

## ISP Cut-off

Most ISPs, mindful of the need to keep their networks as free from congestion as possible, will automatically cut off dial-up connections after a specific period (typically two hours) to prevent overuse. A few don't have a cutoff period at all; it depends on the package you signed up for.

The only real problem that this cutoff issue causes, apart from the nuisance of having to reconnect periodically, is when a large file is being downloaded and the cutoff point comes before the download is completed. You will then have to restart the download from the beginning.

While this problem cannot be eliminated, you can minimize it. The way to do it is with what's known as a download manager. This is a program that monitors a download and, if it is interrupted for any reason, will resume it from the point at which the download stopped. This means you don't have to start again at the beginning. A download manager will also offer other useful features, such as faster download speeds, automatic scheduling, automatic redial and easy-to-see details regarding file size, download time and so on.

*There are various download managers on the market, two popular ones being GetRight and Gozilla. Both of these are easily obtainable from computer magazine cover CDs. You can also download free versions of them from the manufacturers' websites. GetRight is available from getright.com and Gozilla from gozilla.com.*

*NOTE: the free versions of both these applications come with advertisements and reminders.*

The screenshot below is taken from an application of this type called "GetRight" and shows a download in progress.

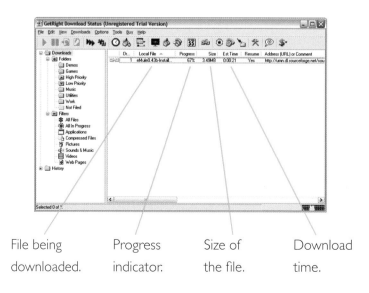

File being downloaded.  Progress indicator.  Size of the file.  Download time.

# Slow Connections

*Network congestion can also affect cable users. Typically, you will be sharing your connection's bandwidth with other local users. This is known as the contention ratio and an average figure is 50:1. This means that 49 other people are also using your connection. If most of them happen to be active simultaneously (browsing, downloading or whatever) your own access times will suffer.*

### Telephone/Cable Line

Swift and reliable network access depends on many factors, and the one most commonly overlooked is the telephone line itself. An obvious indicator of problems in this area is line static; another is if your connection speed is significantly less than it should be.

If you sometimes hear crackling when you use the phone, there is a bad connection on the circuit – contact the phone company and get them to fix it. You can also ask them to increase the "gain" on the line. This basically means the level of signal amplification, and a higher level can make a significant difference.

### Network Congestion

We all know the problem – click on a link and the page takes an eternity to open. The usual cause is congestion. This can be with your ISP or the site itself. If congestion is the problem, you will notice that it occurs mostly in the evenings and at weekends (when everyone else is online as well). There is nothing you can do about this, so either put up with it or try again at another time.

*The issue of graphics is one of the main considerations when it comes to website design. This is worth remembering should you ever decide to build a site or homepage of your own.*

*A well designed site will keep graphic content to the minimum, as most people simply click past a slow-loading page. Take a look at the sites of major corporations: the vast majority of them have few, if any, advertising banners, and links will be text-based rather than graphical.*

### Graphics

Along with sound files, graphics are the slowest-loading element of a web page, and for this reason a site that contains many graphics will take time to open. Plain text is the quickest element; if this is the type of content you wish to access, there is a way to bypass any graphics on the page, which are slowing down access.

1    Go to the Control Panel and open Internet Options.

2    In the Properties dialog box, click the Advanced tab.

3    Scroll down and you will see options to disable animations, sound, videos and images. Disabling these will speed up web page access times significantly.

There is a setting in Internet Options that, when enabled, will automatically clear the browser cache when Internet Explorer is shut down. You can access this by opening Internet Options and clicking the Advanced tab. Scroll down until you see the "Empty Temporary Internet Files Folder when browser is closed" checkbox.

## Browser Cache

If you are having problems with the way some websites load, or if the web seems unusually slow, the problem may be with the browser cache.

This is a folder on your computer where the browser saves copies of visited web pages. It does this so that if you visit the page again it will load faster. In time this folder will fill up with literally thousands of files; a potential consequence of this is that rather than speeding up browsing, as it is intended to do, it will actually slow things down. To prevent this, periodically clear out the cache.

Go to Start, Control Panel and open Internet Options. Under Temporary Internet Files, click Delete files.

If your system is in an unstable condition (see Chapter 9), you could experience problems when surfing the Net. Try rebooting the PC – this will clear the system's memory and close down or reset any service or application that might be causing problems.

If your web browsing is persistently slow, you could need more RAM in your system.

2 Tick the "Delete all offline content" box and then click OK.

## Modem Speed

Have you got your modem revved up? Find out as follows:

1 Go to Start, Control Panel, Phone & Modem Options. Click the Modems tab and then click Properties.

If your modem is an older model, it could well benefit from an upgrade. Visit the manufacturer's website and you should find both a driver and firmware upgrade available for free download.

The firmware upgrade will reprogram your modem and allow it to take advantage of the latest V.92 modem technology.

2 Click the Modem tab and check that the Maximum Port Speed is set to your modem's maximum connection speed.

Spyware gets into a computer by "hitching a ride" on media and software applications downloaded from the Internet. Freeware and Shareware programs are the usual culprits. Also, file-sharing networks such as Kazaa are rife with them.

If you are getting very slow download speeds when downloading from file-sharing networks (Emule, Kazaa, etc.) be aware that many ISPs will put a block on the port being used by the application. They do this because frequent use of file-sharing programs places a heavy load on their bandwidth.

You can usually get round this by choosing a different port in the program.

If you have not yet updated to Windows XP Service Pack 2, and you are having problems with your current version of Internet Explorer, take the opportunity to do so now.

Rather than reinstalling it as described opposite, download and install SP2. Alternatively, you can order it on a free CD from Microsoft.

## Spyware

These are programs that are surreptitiously downloaded to a user's computer and which then gather information about the user and relay it to advertisers or other interested parties. Typically, the type of information looked for is the user's web browsing habits (such as what type of sites they commonly visit). More sophisticated spyware programs can actually redirect a browser to specific sites (see page 152 for more on this).

This practice is now so widespread that there are probably very few home PCs that don't have numerous spyware programs installed on them. As they work by hijacking your Internet connection to report back to their makers, the more of these you have on your system, the slower your connection will be.

The solution is to download and run a spyware detection program such as Ad-aware from www.lavasoftusa.com. This scans your system for the presence of spyware and then uninstalls it.

Spyware programs detected by Ad-aware.

## Corrupted or Misconfigured Browser

Internet Explorer 6 is a highly complex piece of software and as such is prone to errors and configuration issues. If you are having problems when browsing the web, and all else fails, try reinstalling it:

Place the XP installation disc in the CD drive.

Then go to Start, Run. In the Run box, type the following:
rundll32.exe setupapi,InstallHinfSection DefaultInstall 132 %windir%\Inf\ie.inf

Click OK and Internet Explorer will now be reinstalled. Alternatively, you can try the method described on page 170.

# Unable To Access Certain Sites

There is a lot of unpleasant stuff on the web and this is a serious concern for any responsible parent.

Windows Content Advisor, while not being the best application of it's type, does allow a degree of censorship. You can, for example, create a list of websites that can be viewed by your family. If your kids attempt to access a website that is not on your approved list, they will be prompted for the Content Advisor Supervisor password to proceed.

However, dedicated censorship programs such as Net Nanny and Cyber Patrol offer many more options and provide a much higher level of protection.

If you have enabled the Content Advisor, have set a password for it but forgotten what it is, you can delete it by doing the following:

1) Open the registry editor by typing regedit in the Start menu Run box.

2) Locate the following key: HKEY_LOCAL_MACHINE\ Software\Microsoft\Windows\ Current Version\Policies\Ratings.

3) In the right-hand window, you will see an entry labeled Key. Right-click this and click Delete. The password will now be removed.

There any number of reasons why you may not be able to access a certain website. The following are the most common.

## Site Congested

Popular sites, such as the Microsoft site, can at times become extremely congested with thousands of users all trying to get in to it at the same time. Eventually, the browser will give up and display a "Page cannot be displayed" error message. About the only thing you can do in this situation is to try again later.

## Firewalls

It's worth noting here that a firewall's default settings are extremely unlikely to be ideal for any one particular setup and can, and often do, cause all sorts of connection problems, including site access. If you are having access problems and have a firewall installed, try disabling it and see if the problem clears: if it does, then you need to set it up correctly. Read the manufacturer's instructions or visit one of the many specialist websites.

## Content Advisor

This is Microsoft's attempt to provide an Internet content censorship facility. Not being the best application of its type, it will, unfortunately, also block access to sites with absolutely no offensive content. Check it out by doing the following:

1 Click Internet Options in the Control Panel. Click the Content tab and then click Enable.

2 Drag the slider to adjust the level of censorship.

*The main purpose of cookies is to identify users and their preferences when browsing a particular site. For example, cookies can be used to remember log-in names and passwords, so that users do not need to reregister every time they visit a site.*

*You can delete cookies from your PC by opening Internet Options and clicking Delete Cookies.*

## Cookies

A cookie is basically a small text file of information specific to a user, which is given to their web browser by a website when that site is visited. The message is then sent back to the site each time the user opens a page from the site in future visits.

This is all innocuous stuff, which takes place in the background and needn't be of any concern to the user. The problems come when a user, either intentionally or accidently, restricts cookie acceptance in his or her browser.

This is because some sites will refuse access if they are unable to place their cookie on a user's PC. So, if you find you can access most sites without a problem, but there are some you can't, you need to investigate how your browser is set up to handle cookies. Do this as described below:

1   Go to the Control Panel and click Internet Options. Then click the Privacy tab. The following dialog box will open.

*If the cookie level is already set to Medium (step 2 opposite), do the following:*

*1) Click the Advanced button.*

*2) In the Additional Privacy Settings dialog box, select Override Automatic Cookie Handling.*

*3) Click Accept under both First Party Cookies and Third Party Cookies. Then click OK.*

2   Make sure the slider is not set to Block All Cookies. If it is, then drag it down to Medium.

3   If you're not sure what level of protection you need, then click the Default button.

Having a higher than necessary level of cookie protection can also result in problems when accessing certain pages in a website. A typical example of this is password-protected pages, which might not open at all.

# Miscellaneous Internet Issues

*There are three causes of script debugging error messages: Firstly, the web page author has made a programming error. Secondly, you may be running a pop-up blocker that closes pop-up windows so fast that the script on the web page fails. Thirdly, you might have some adware or spyware installed on your computer that activates the script error messages.*

*When Internet Explorer detects an error on a page, it launches a script debugger to diagnose the problem. Whenever one of the messages appear, always choose No from the options.*

*Java is a programming language, developed for the Internet, which enables small applications (known as applets) to be run from web pages. These can be literally anything – digital clocks, animated figures, calendars, etc. However, before Java applets will work, a Java Virtual Machine must be installed.*

*Download the Sun Microsystems Virtual Machine from www. java.com/en/ download/windows_automatic.jsp. This works just as well as Microsoft's version.*

## Script Debugging Error Messages

A common problem that can occur when browsing the Internet with Internet Explorer is the sudden appearance of "Script Debug" error messages. These usually say something like "Script error at line 01. Do you wish to debug?" These messages can be persistent and extremely irritating.

Get rid of them as follows:

Go to Start, Control Panel and Internet Options.

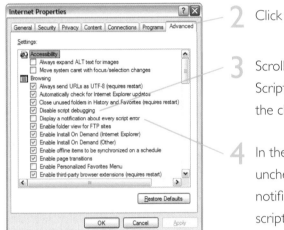

2 Click the Advanced tab.

3 Scroll down to Disable Script Debugging and tick the checkbox.

4 In the same dialog box, uncheck the "Display a notification about every script error" checkbox.

## Java Virtual Machine

You click on a link in a website and receive a message stating that the Microsoft Java Virtual Machine needs to be installed. The message also contains a download link. However, when you click this you get another message saying that the Microsoft Java Virtual Machine is no longer available for download. So what gives?

The reason the link doesn't work is that Microsoft and Sun Microsystems, who each have their own version of the Java Virtual Machine, are currently engaged in a legal wrangle over this application. Microsoft have withdrawn their version until this is resolved.

The solution to this is simple – download it from another source, such as web.ivtasp.com/qa/hotfoot/msjavx86.exe.

*There is another way of disabling browser pop-ups. Go to Internet Options and click the Security tab. Then click the Custom Levels button. In the new dialog box, scroll down and tick Disable Active Scripting.*

*NOTE: This might cause some websites to be displayed incorrectly.*

## Browser Pop-up Windows

If used for the right purpose, such as displaying useful information, pop-up windows are an acceptable part of browsing the Internet. Unfortunately, however, they are all too often used to display irritating ads and other such stuff. The solution to this problem is to use a pop-up blocker.

One that I recommend comes with the Google Toolbar – a useful browser add-on in itself. You can download this from http://toolbar.google.com.

Toggle the Google pop-up blocker on and off.

*Many of the latest firewall and anti-virus programs also offer pop-up blockers; for example, Norton has one.*

Alternatively, install Windows XP SP2. This adds a pop-up blocker to Internet Explorer.

## Homepage Hijacks

There are many sites that will override your browser's homepage setting and install themselves as the homepage. When you fire up your browser, you will automatically be taken to the site in question. Resolve this as described below:

*If you find that your attempts to reset a hijacked homepage are continuously blocked, then you have a more severe form of hijacking known as browser hijacking. This can usually be resolved by downloading and running a program such as Ad-aware, which is available from www.lavasoftusa.com.*

*There is also a particularly virulent browser hijacking program currently running amok on the Internet. This is known as CWS and details of this are on the next page.*

1 Open Internet Options in the Control Panel.

2 Under Home Page, click Use Blank.

3 Internet Explorer will now open a blank page. Alternatively, you can specify a site of your own choice by entering its address in the box.

*CoolWebSearch is not a virus, as it does not replicate itself. Rather, it is what's known as a Trojan. These can be just as destructive as viruses.*

*The program originates from a company in Russia and redirects to a pay-per-click search engine. Since its inception in 2003, it is estimated to have accumulated over 1000 affiliates, all with their own sites.*

*CoolWebSearch gets on to a computer system by exploiting a security loophole in the Microsoft Virtual Machine.*

*You can prevent CWS from getting on your system by uninstalling the Microsoft Virtual Machine and replacing it with Sun Microsystem's Virtual Machine. Alternatively, install XP Service Pack 2.*

*Operating Systems affected by CWS are: Windows 95, Windows 98, Windows NT, Windows 2000, Windows XP and Windows Me. CWS and its variants will not affect Windows 3.x, Macintosh, OS/2, UNIX, or Linux.*

# Browser Hijacks

While having your homepage hijacked may be irritating, it is nothing compared to having your browser taken over completely, to the extent that it controls you rather than vice versa.

This is what will happen should you be unfortunate enough to be hit with a browser hijacking program called CoolWebSearch, also known as CWS. This thoroughly nasty piece of software appeared in the summer of 2003 and is now considered to be one of the most invasive and devious browser hijackers in existence. It can manifest itself in any of the following ways:

- A new toolbar suddenly appears in your browser. Internet Explorer slows to a crawl.
- All web searches are redirected to other sites – usually porn or advertising sites. You have no control over your browser.
- Users' homepages are reset to Smartsearch.ws (or variants) and all attempts to remove this are blocked.
- You get a continuous assault of porn pop-up windows.
- Porn and advertising sites are bookmarked in Internet Favorites.
- There is a marked decrease in overall PC performance.

So, what can you do should you find yourself with this pestilence on your computer? About the only way to remove the worst variants of CWS is with a program called CoolWebShredder, and even this is not guaranteed to work. Download it from www.spywareinfo.com/~merijn.

If you are unfortunate enough not to be able to remove CWS from your system – and many people aren't – a reformat of the hard disk followed by a clean installation of XP could be your only remaining option. See pages 56–57 for instructions on this.

Finally, if you think your anti-virus software will protect you from CWS and its many mutations, think on. While it will stop some, it won't stop them all. CoolWebSearch is an extremely insidious application and many variants of it have the ability to automatically mutate themselves by changing their own source code. New CWS variants are being detected on a weekly basis and the majority of anti-virus programs can do little, if anything, to stop them from infecting a system.

# Setting Up an Email Account

At the risk of stating the obvious, you need to be connected to the Internet before you can use a PC's email facility. Emails don't appear by magic, they need a physical route to and from your computer.

While the set up procedures detailed in this section are specific to Outlook Express 6, the actual settings will be much the same whichever email application you are using.

You can also use the program's help file should you feel the need. Alternatively, all email programs will have an account set-up wizard, which will help you to fill in all the required settings. Open Outlook Express's wizard by clicking Accounts from the Tools menu. Then click Add and, from the menu, select Mail.

To check that your email account is working, simply send yourself an email. Alternatively, some email programs (not including Outlook Express), have a test facility, which will check all the necessary settings and also send and receive a test email to confirm that everything is working correctly. If you are using Outlook, as opposed to Outlook Express, you will have this option available.

Before we go any further, we will assume that you have a working Internet connection. This immediately eliminates your Network Connection software as a potential cause of problems.

Most problems regarding the sending and receiving of electronic mail are caused by incorrect settings in associated applications. For this reason, we will begin this section with a detailed explanation of how to correctly set up email software. As this is a book focused on XP, we will use the email program bundled with it: Outlook Express.

Start Outlook Express and then carry out the following procedure:

1 From the Tools menu, click Accounts and then click the Mail tab.

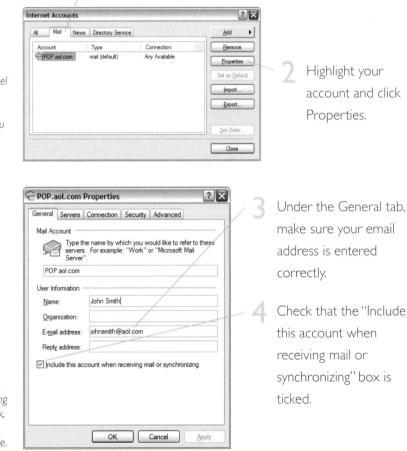

2 Highlight your account and click Properties.

3 Under the General tab, make sure your email address is entered correctly.

4 Check that the "Include this account when receiving mail or synchronizing" box is ticked.

*Many people are confused by the issue of POP and SMTP server settings. These stand for "Post Office Protocol" and "Simple Mail Transfer Protocol" respectively.*

*Basically, they are Internet languages used for the transmission (SMTP) and reception (POP) of email messages. It is essential that they are entered correctly in the email software.*

*If you are in any doubt as to what the correct POP and SMTP settings should be, a quick phone call to your ISP will give you the answer.*

*Before you do, though, try entering the ISP's name, e.g. POP.aol.com, as demonstrated in the screenshot opposite.*

*Ticking the "Remember password" box in the Email Account Properties dialog box, will eliminate the need to enter it manually each time you open Outlook Express.*

*Also, as you can't actually see what password is entered in the password box, delete the current entry and then reenter it to make sure it's correct.*

5 Click the Servers tab.

**POP.aol.com Properties**

General | Servers | Connection | Security | Advanced

Server Information
My incoming mail server is a [POP3] server.
Incoming mail (POP3): POP.aol.com
Outgoing mail (SMTP): SMTP.aol.com

Incoming Mail Server
Account name: johnsmith
Password: ••••
☑ Remember password
☐ Log on using Secure Password Authentication

Outgoing Mail Server
☐ My server requires authentication  [Settings...]

[OK] [Cancel] [Apply]

6 Check that your POP3 and SMTP settings are correct. Contact your ISP if in any doubt.

7 Check that your Account name and Password are correct. Delete the password and enter it again to be sure.

Your Outlook Express account has now been correctly set up. Before you start though, make sure you have the following information to hand:

- The type of email server you use – POP3 (most email accounts), HTTP (such as Hotmail), or IMAP.

- The name of the incoming email server.

- For POP3 and IMAP servers, the name of the outgoing email server (generally SMTP).

- Your account name and password.

- Does your ISP require you to use Secure Password Authentication (SPA) to access your email account?

# Problems With Receiving Email

*Don't overlook the possibility that the attachment is corrupt. This could have happened at the source or during the download to your PC. Usually, in this situation, you will get an error message of some description. If you suspect this to be the problem, contact the sender and ask them to send the file again.*

*Outlook Express's Security settings are designed to prevent users inadvertently opening email attachments that could potentially be carrying a virus. If the attachment you are attempting to open is of a type that Outlook Express considers to be dangerous, by default it won't allow it to be opened.*

*However, you can get a good idea yourself by having a look at the attachment's file extension: if it is .exe, .com, .bat, .pif, .scr or .vbs, be wary. These extensions belong to programs and scripts that can carry viruses. Do not open any of these without first scanning them with a virus checker.*

*Extensions such as .gif and .wav belong to image and sound files and are quite safe. If the extension is .doc or .xls, the file is a Microsoft Office document, which may contain macros. These have the potential to be dangerous.*

## Attachments Won't Open

You click on a file attached to an email you've received and nothing happens. The usual causes of this problem are:

You don't have the necessary software installed on your PC with which to open the file. For example, a spreadsheet file created with Microsoft Excel will not open unless you have Excel on your system. In this situation XP will give you a "Windows cannot open this file" error message, as shown in the screenshot below:

The Web service option takes you to a site called cknow, from where you will be able to identify the program used to create the file.

2 The "Select the program from a list" option will be of use only if the file in question can be opened by a different program on the PC.

This problem can also be caused by your Security settings in Outlook Express. Check it out as follows:

In Outlook Express, click Options from the Tools menu. Click the Security tab.

2 Uncheck "Do not allow attachments to be saved or opened that could potentially be a virus."

## Emails Take Ages to Download

Most messages take just a few seconds to download to a PC. Some, though, can take much longer, and people who aren't too familiar with email might suspect something is wrong with their setup.

However, the cause of this is nothing to do with the computer or its Internet connection; rather, it is due to the size of the email message – the bigger it is, the longer it will take to download. You will usually find in these cases that the person who created the message also included media content, such as images and video.

If you don't want this to happen again, the solution is to create a message rule that will prevent the download of any messages over a specified size. You can do this by selecting Message Rules, Mail, from the Tools tab in Outlook Express.

## Unable to Download Email

If you are unable to download any email at all, the cause could lie with any firewall or anti-virus programs you have installed. Applications of this type will usually have an option to block the reception of all email. Although it won't be enabled by default, it could have been set inadvertently, so check it out.

This problem can also be caused by settings in Outlook Express's Message Rules, particularly if you find that certain emails are received while others aren't. Message Rules enable a user to place restrictions on received messages; for example, all emails from specific users, or over a specified size, can be blocked.

*XP comes with a handy utility that will automatically reduce the size of an image file to make it suitable for emailing. All you have to do is right-click the image file and click Send To. Click Mail Recipient and a dialog box will open offering you several resizing options. Make your choice and then click OK. XP will now open a new message window in your default email program, with the resized image attached. Add the recipient's address and type in your message text. Then click Send.*

*Many ISP's will not forward email messages over a certain size. If you know a message has been sent to you, but it didn't arrive, it could be worth contacting your ISP to see whether they have a size limit on emails.*

*Outlook Express's Message Rules give you many options on how to handle incoming emails. For example, rules can be created to delete a message, move or copy them to a specified folder, not download from the server (ISP) and even delete them from the server.*

From the Tools menu click Message Rules, Mail. If you have any rules, they will be displayed in the Message Rules dialog box, together with a description of the selected rule.

# Problems With Sending Email

*Server timeout problems are much more likely to happen with a dial-up connection than with a cable connection. This is because connection speeds are much slower with a dial-up setup.*

## Server Timeouts

If your attempts to send messages frequently fail and you get timeout error messages, adjust your timeout settings as follows:

1   In Outlook Express go to Tools, Accounts. Highlight your account, and click Properties. In the next dialog box, click the Advanced tab.

2   Drag the slider to increase the Server Timeout period. This specifies how long Outlook Express will wait for a response from the server before stopping an attempt to send an email. NOTE: Server timeout problems can also occur when receiving email.

*Server Authentication is necessary only when an email account is set up with a server that requires it. Typically, these can be university campuses and government departments.*

*These types of organization will usually only accept emails from users authorized by the organization in question.*

*However, if a user attempts to send a message to a server that doesn't require authentication, but the user does have it enabled, an error message will result.*

## Server Authentication

If you get a "Server rejected your login with Secure Password Authentication" error message when trying to send an email, do the following:

1   From the Tools menu, click Accounts. Select your account and click Properties. Then click the Servers tab.

2   In the dialog box that opens, remove the check mark from the "My server requires authentication" checkbox.

# Outlook Express Issues

## Outlook Express Automatically Closes the Connection

A common problem users experience with Outlook Express is when the program automatically shuts down the Internet connection once it has finished sending and receiving messages.

To rectify this, do the following:

By default, Outlook Express is configured to check automatically for emails waiting to be downloaded. To do this it needs to be connected, and so will dial your connection. Similarly, if you have any messages in your Outbox, it will attempt to send these as well. This can be extremely irritating if all you want to do is look at existing messages or maybe write a new one offline.

Another problem caused by Outlook Express's automatic dial feature comes when you have different connections for your Internet and email. This is because Internet Explorer also has an automatic dial feature.

If both of these are enabled, you will find that when already connected to the Internet, launching Internet Explorer or Outlook Express causes the activated program to attempt to disconnect from the current connection and reconnect to another one.

Prevent Outlook Express doing this as described opposite. For Internet Explorer, go to Control Panel and open Internet Options. Click the Connections tab and tick the "Never Dial a Connection" box.

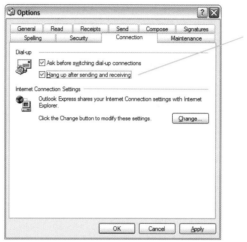

From the Tools menu, click Options and then the Connection tab. Uncheck the "Hang up after sending and receiving" box.

## Outlook Express Automatically Dials When Opened

Another common problem is when Outlook Express automatically dials your connection when it is opened. This prevents users from being able to compose their messages offline. Fix it as follows:

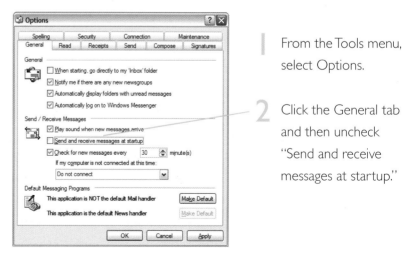

From the Tools menu, select Options.

2 Click the General tab and then uncheck "Send and receive messages at startup."

## Outlook Express Keeps Prompting For A Password

Your password is not retained even though you have configured Outlook Express to save it. This is a known issue with Outlook Express and XP, which relates to a damaged registry key. Resolve it as follows:

*To start the registry editor, go to Start, Run and then type regedit in the Run box.*

1 In the registry editor (see tip), locate the following registry key: HKEY_CURRENT_USER\Software\Microsoft\Protected Storage System Provider

2 Right-click the key and then select Permissions.

3 In the dialog box, click the Advanced tab. Tick "Replace permission entries…" and click OK. In the next dialog box click Yes.

4 Repeat steps 2 through 4 for each subkey that is listed under the Protected Storage System Provider registry key.

5 At this point, you can now delete the Protected Storage System Provider key by clicking Delete on the Edit menu.

6 Start Outlook Express. When Outlook Express checks your email account you will be able to reenter your password.

# How to Deal With Spam

Another method of reducing the amount of spam you receive is to use Outlook Express's Blocked Senders utility. This allows you to place a block on all messages from a specified sender.

Access this by going to Tools, Message Rules and clicking Blocked Senders list. Click the Blocked Senders tab and then Add. This opens a dialog box for you to enter an address from which you do not want to receive emails. There is no limit to the number of addresses you can block in this way.

You can get a spammer's address from the "From" line at the top of the message, although this may have been faked.

Don't be fooled by phrases such as "to be removed from this list, click here." Spammers use phrases like this to entice users to respond to the emails. Doing so tells the spammer that your email address is valid and reaches a real person. This will be valuable to them because they can then sell your address with the assurance that the email address is legitimate.

If you need to give an email address in order to access a specific web page, just enter a false invalid one. In most cases it won't make the slightest difference, apart from keeping your Inbox clear that is.

Unsolicited email is a problem that can quite literally be described as a plague. Currently, it is estimated that approximately half of all emails worldwide are due to the spammers. Furthermore, this percentage is growing year by year.

In order to prevent yourself falling victim to the spammers, you need to know how they get hold of email addresses in the first place. One of the favorite methods is to use special software that trawls the web for email addresses; as these all contain the "@" symbol, they are easy to identify. Once a list is compiled, it is sold to advertising companies.

Many websites exist specifically to collect email addresses. They are disguised in any number of ways, but the one thing they all have in common is that to access anything you will first need to enter your email address. Most websites offering free downloads, often including those of major corporations, will require a visitor to enter an email address before they can access the download page. Newsgroups, forums, and chatrooms, where users need to post their email address in order to receive a reply, are another favorite source. Even offline stores are getting in on the act. For example, you might be asked to fill in a questionnaire, one of which will just happen to concern your email address.

So, if you don't wish to receive spam, the solution is simply never to give out your address to anyone you don't wish to receive messages from.

However, if this advice comes too late and your inbox is already bulging at the seams with unsolicited trash, here are a couple of things you can do.

The first thing is to simply delete the email account and open a new one with a new address: most ISPs give you the option to have several. Box clever this time, and only give the new address to people you can trust.

You can also make use of Outlook Express's Message Rules utility. This won't stop all spam, but will block much of it.

# Miscellaneous XP Problems Troubleshooting

This chapter is devoted to a miscellaneous selection of problems that are specific to Windows XP.

## Covers

**Chapter Fourteen**

# XP Keeps Asking For A Password

Every time you start your PC, instead of Windows going straight to the Desktop, it stops with a log-on dialog box requesting a password, as shown in the screenshot below.

*If you make a habit of downloading and installing XP updates, as you should, beware of one particular update called Microsoft .Net Framework 1.1. Without going into the reasons here, this will automatically setup a new user account, which will undo the procedure described on this page.*

To get to the Desktop you have to enter a password and then click OK.

Should you not require this, or find it a nuisance, you can get rid of the log-on box as follows:

2 Go to Start, Control Panel, User Accounts. At the first dialog box click "Change the way users log on or off."

*If you need more than one account, but want XP to go straight to the Desktop, you need to install TweakUI. You can download this from the Microsoft website, and when it is installed you can access it from the All Programs menu. Open TweakUI and then click on Autologon. Check the box titled "Log on automatically at system startup," enter your user name and password and click OK. Now TweakUI will automatically log you on using your user name and password, even if more than one account exists.*

3 Remove the check mark from the Use the Welcome screen checkbox.

However, while steps 2 to 3 above will eliminate the log-on box, you may still find Windows stops at the Welcome screen with a list of the currently active user accounts. To get to the desktop you have to click the account you wish to run.

If you don't want this either, you will have to delete all the accounts apart from the main account and the guest account. To do this open User Accounts as described in step 2, but this time click "Change an Account." Click the relevant accounts in turn and click "Delete this account." You will also need to ensure that the main and guest accounts aren't password-protected.

# Desktop Spam Messages

A problem that many users new to XP soon encounter, particularly those that have broadband connections, is that of unsolicited spam messages periodically popping up on the desktop.

The Messenger Service is intended for use by system administrators to notify Windows users about their networks. However, many advertisers are abusing this service to send spam.

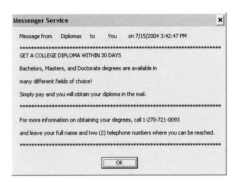

Although the name is similar, XP's Messenger Service is not related to Windows Messenger. Disabling Windows Messenger will not prevent Messenger Service spam on your computer. The Messenger Service provides no useful purpose to users and so can be safely disabled.

These messages are transmitted via XP's Messenger Service and to get rid of them permanently, you need to disable the Messenger Service. Do it as follows:

Go to Start, Control Panel and click Administrative Tools. Then click Services. Locate the Messenger Service and double-click it.

As an alternative to disabling the Messenger Service, you can enable XP's Internet Connection Firewall (enabled by default on Windows XP SP2). This blocks the ports required for Messenger Service data transmission.

2 In Messenger Properties, select Disabled.

3 Stop the Service by clicking Stop.

If you have a broadband connection, it's also a good move to enable XP's Internet Connection Firewall.

# Private Folders Option is Unavailable

XP provides users with the facility to make folders private so that other users cannot see the contents. To do it you right-click a folder and then click the Sharing tab. You then see a dialog box, which gives you the option to make the folder private.

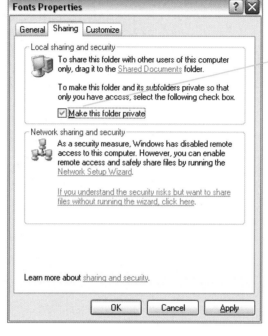

Tick the "Make this folder private" checkbox.

However, many people who try this discover that the option is grayed out and thus not available. The usual reason for this is the fact that the hard disk must be formatted with the NTFS file system. If your disk is FAT formatted, you cannot make folders private.

If this is the situation, you do have the option to convert to NTFS, which is a straightforward process. Before you do so though, be aware that doing this is a one-way ticket: once your system is converted to NTFS, there is no way of going back to FAT unless you are prepared to reformat your disk and then reinstall XP (see pages 56–57). However, unless you are running a dual-boot setup that includes a previous version of Windows, there is no reason not to be using NTFS anyway.

To convert your file system to NTFS, do the following:

Go to Start, All Programs, Accessories, Command Prompt.

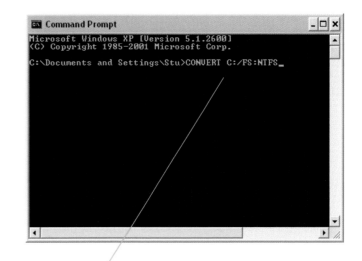

At the prompt type CONVERT C: /FS:NTFS and hit Enter

The PC will now reboot and the conversion process will begin.

The other common cause of the "Make folder private" option being grayed out is that the user is trying to do it on a folder that cannot be made private. This change can only be made to folders that are in your user profile; these include My Documents, Desktop, Start Menu, Cookies, and Favorites.

So if you want a folder in which to keep your private data, you must create it within your user profile folder or one of the existing subfolders (such as My Documents).

The only exception to this is the Desktop: you can make any folder on your Desktop private, as the desktop files are stored in the Desktop folder within the User Profile folder.

You can access your User Profile folder by opening your C drive and clicking Documents and Settings.

# Delayed Write Failed Errors

This appears to be quite a common problem with XP, and occurs during file transfer operations. The term itself – Delayed Write Failed – is quite meaningless to most people and is more sensibly defined as data corruption.

The problem will announce itself with a yellow pop-up message over the taskbar as shown below.

*This problem can also be caused by a faulty hard disk or incompatible hard disk controller drivers. Visit your hard disk manufacturer's website and download the latest driver for the controller.*

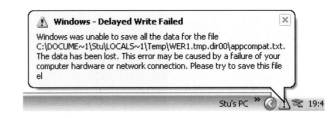

As data corruption can be caused by any number of things, there is no easy answer to this. You can, however, try the following:

*You can also try defragmenting your hard drive. A heavily fragmented drive is often the cause of file transfer errors.*

1   Open My Computer, right-click the hard disk and select Properties. Click the Hardware tab, click the hard disk, and then click the Properties tab. Finally, click the Policies tab.

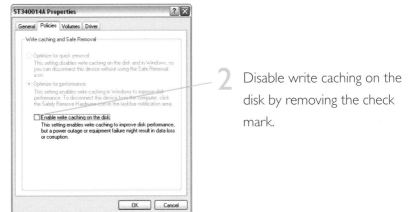

2   Disable write caching on the disk by removing the check mark.

Write caching is a means of improving hard disk performance by using a "buffer" zone to temporarily store data during the write process. However, in certain circumstances it can be the cause of data corruption and hence delayed write errors.

# Password Expiration

This page is for those of you running XP Professional; it does not apply to XP Home.

After you have been running Windows XP Pro for a while, you may receive this message when you log on: "Your password will expire in 14 days."

As a security measure, by default, XP will not allow passwords to run longer than 42 days. 14 days in advance of expiry, XP will start warning you of this fact. However, if you are quite happy with your existing passwords, you can prevent this, as described below:

For those of you with poor memories, here's a good tip for making sure you never forget your log-on password. XP enables a user to create a Password Recovery Disk. Do it as follows:
1) Open User Accounts in the Control Panel.
2) Select the account for which you want to create a Password Recovery Disk.
3) From the Related Tasks at the left-hand side, choose "Prevent a forgotten password."
4) Follow the wizard's instructions to create the recovery disk.
If and when you forget your password, you will see a link to use your Password Recovery Disk. This will verify your access rights and prompt you to create a new password, which will enable you to access your account. The new password is written to your recovery disk at the same time as you create it.

1  Go to Start, Run and in the Run box type *control userpasswords2*

2  Select the Advanced tab in the User Accounts dialog box.

3  Click the Advanced button below the Advanced User Management header.

4  Select Users in the Local Users and Groups.

5  In the right pane, right-click the user name for which you want to change the setting, and select Properties.

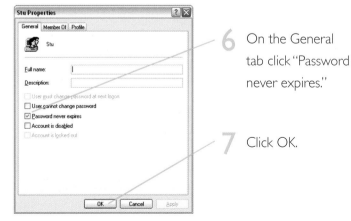

6  On the General tab click "Password never expires."

7  Click OK.

Your passwords will now never expire.

# XP Keeps Rebooting

A problem that many people have with XP is unexpected reboots. You can be happily engaged in whatever it is that you do on your PC and then suddenly, with absolutely no warning, it reboots. This can happen only occasionally or, in the worst cases, continuously.

The cause of this is that XP has run into a problem – in Microsoft parlance, a stop error. In previous versions of Windows this would result in the dreaded "blue screen of death."

XP, however, considers that such errors could place data at risk and so immediately reboots the system rather than continuing on and possibly corrupting data. The first thing to do is stop this automatic rebooting.

1 Go to Start, Control Panel and System. Click the Advanced tab and then, under Startup and Recovery, click Settings.

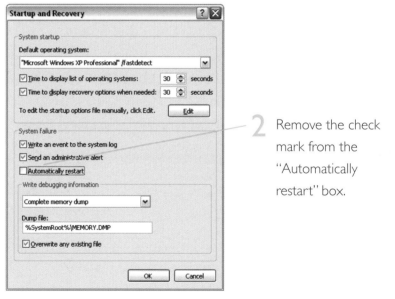

2 Remove the check mark from the "Automatically restart" box.

Now when Windows XP encounters a stop Error, it will simply display an error message. If the problem is persistent, you will have to find out the cause: the usual suspects are device drivers and incompatible third-party software.

# XP's Backup Won't Record to Disc

XP's backup utility is a law unto itself. Microsoft really haven't made this an easy feature to use. The first problem that users of XP Home will have is finding the thing in the first place. Previous versions of Windows made it available from the Programs menu: Not so XP. For reasons known best to themselves, Microsoft have seen fit to leave the backup utility on the XP installation disc – it isn't installed by default. To install it yourself, do the following:

*Microsoft's explanation is that XP's Removable Storage Management does not recognize CD-R, CD-RW, or DVD-R devices as backup media, even though you can specify these media types in Removable Storage Management. Ntbackup.exe therefore does not support backup to these devices. Removable Storage Management regards CD-R, CD-RW, or DVD-R as just a file-system-capable media type. However, as the Windows file system does not support formatting CD-R, CD-RW, or DVD-R media, Removable Storage Management cannot write an RSM free label because the disc appears to be write-protected. This means that Removable Storage Management treats CD-R, CD-RW, and DVD-R media as read-only media types.*

1. Dig out the XP CD and insert it in the CD-ROM drive.

2. Open My Computer, right-click the CD drive and click Open. You will now see the contents of the disc.

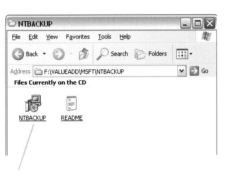

3. Click the ValueAdd folder, then the MSFT folder and finally the NTBackup folder.

4. Click NTBACKUP to install XP's backup utility.

The backup program will now be available from All Programs, Accessories, System Tools.

*There are plenty of much better backup programs on the market. Indeed, quite a few can be found on the Internet – some of these are available as free downloads.*

Now comes the next surprise. Having selected the data you wish to back up, you then specify your CD writer as the backup medium (as you can with virtually all other backup programs). However, when you click the Save button, the utility just gives you a message saying it cannot use the file name and that the file path is invalid.

The clue is in the README file on the CD (shown in the screenshot above). This will inform you that the backup utility is not designed to record to CDs or DVDs. The only thing you can do with it is save your backup as a file on the hard drive and then burn it to disc with disc mastering software.

# Repairing Internet Explorer 6

*Another way of repairing Internet Explorer is to download it from the Microsoft website. Go to: www.microsoft.com/windows/ie/ downloads/critical/ie6sp1/ default.asp. However, if you are on a dial-up connection this is perhaps not so feasible, as the download will be approximately 25 MB.*

*Alternatively, you can order it from Microsoft on a CD, providing you live in the USA or Canada.*

A number of XP users have reported situations whereby Internet Explorer 6 has become corrupted, resulting in error messages and faults of various types.

Unlike most software, which can simply be reinstalled from a CD in a short time, Internet Explorer is actually tightly integrated with XP and thus cannot be repaired in this manner. There is however, a way to do it:

1 Place the XP installation disc in the CD drive.

2 Go to Start and click Search. Under "What do you want to search for" click "All files and folders."

3 In the top box type *ie.inf*

4 Select More Advanced Options and place a checkmark beside the Search Hidden Files and Folders option.

*If you have Windows XP Service Pack 2 installed on your system then you already have the latest version of Internet Explorer – this is integrated into SP2.*

5 Ensure that the Search System Folders and Search Subfolders box is also checked.

6 In the Look In drop-down menu, select the letter of the hard drive that contains the Windows folder (usually C). Then click Search.

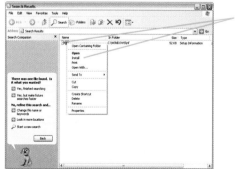

*To find out which version of Internet Explorer you are currently using, open it and, from the Help menu, click About Internet Explorer.*

7 When you see the ie.inf file in the search results, right-click it and then click Install.

8 Internet Explorer will now be reinstalled from the XP CD.

When the file transfer is complete, reboot the computer.

# Restarting Windows Explorer

From time to time, Windows Explorer – which is the application responsible for the Taskbar, Desktop and Start Menu – will crash. The result is that the taskbar and all the desktop icons will disappear leaving a completely blank screen. When this happens there is little a user can do (as there is nothing to click) apart from pressing Ctrl+Alt+Del to open the Task Manager. From the Task Manager's Shutdown menu, the PC can be restarted.

However, there is a better way to recover from this that doesn't involve restarting the computer. The next time Windows Explorer crashes, do the following:

Press Ctrl+Alt+Del to open the Task Manager.

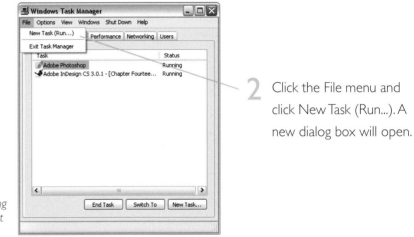

2 Click the File menu and click New Task (Run...). A new dialog box will open.

3 In the Open box, type Explorer and then click OK.

XP will now restart Windows Explorer, which will in turn reinstate the Taskbar, Start menu and the Desktop icons.

# XP's Picture Viewer has Taken Over

If Windows Picture and Fax Viewer insists on opening all your pictures when you'd rather open them with a program of your own choice, then do the following:

*Windows Picture and Fax Viewer is XP's imaging program, and is about as basic as a program of this type can be. Most users will prefer to use something with more features to view their graphics.*

*Unfortunately, because it is installed as the default imaging program, most popular image formats (such as JPEG, TIFF and GIF) will be automatically opened by the Picture and Fax Viewer, even if you have installed another program.*

Right-click an image that has a file type you want to associate with your program.

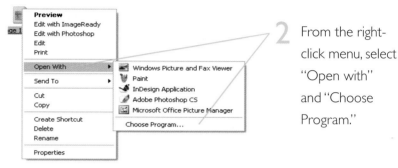

From the right-click menu, select "Open with" and "Choose Program."

The Open With dialog box will now open.

*A much better imaging program is IrfanView, available as a free download from any general download site. This offers many more options and is very simple to use.*

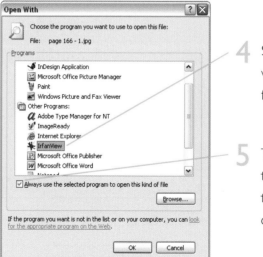

Select the program you wish to use to open the file.

Tick the "Always use the selected program to open this kind of file" checkbox.

Using the example above, from now on the selected image file type will always open with IrfanView. Should you ever wish to use a different program to open it, repeat steps 1 to 5.

# Images Download Only as Bitmaps

A similar issue may be experienced by users of AOL. Images saved with the AOL browser will be in the ART format.

This, however, has nothing to do with the Temporary Internet Files cache. It is, in fact, done by design.

One feature of the AOL software is that, in an effort to speed up browsing, all images are compressed and converted to AOL's ART image format. This feature is enabled by default. The problem with this is that these ART images never look as good as the original image, and furthermore, are incompatible with most imaging software. The solution is to disable the ART compression feature, which you can do as follows:

Go to Preferences on the AOL tool bar and select WWW. Then go to Web Graphics. Uncheck the box that says "Use compressed graphics." Restart AOL for the change to take effect.

When you click "Save Picture As" for a graphics file in Internet Explorer, you may find you have the option to save the file as only a BMP, even if the file is in another format such as GIF or JPEG.

This is a common problem and is usually caused by the Temporary Internet Files cache having been filled to its capacity. Resolve this as follows:

1 Go to Start, Control Panel and Internet Options. Make sure the General tab is open.

2 In the Temporary Internet Files section, click the Delete Files button. This will clear the cache.

3 Alternatively, click the Settings button.

Be careful when increasing the size of your browser cache if you are low on hard disk space. Even if the browser doesn't use it, the space will not be available to other applications.

4 In the dialog box that opens you have the option to increase the size of the cache by dragging the slider. You can use this option if you don't want to delete the existing cache files.

# Recovering Lost Emails

*Users of Outlook Express do not, unfortunately, have access to an email repair tool. The best option here is to create a backup of your email data in case of future problems. Make a backup as follows:*

1) *On the Tools menu, click Options.*
2) *On the Maintenance tab, click Store Folder.*
3) *Highlight the folder location, right-click and click Copy.*
4) *Click Cancel and then click Cancel again to close the dialog box.*
5) *Click Start, and then click Run.*
6) *In the Open box, right-click and click Paste. Click OK.*
7) *Outlook Express's storage folder will now open. On the Edit menu, click Select All.*
8) *On the Edit menu again, click Copy, and then close the window.*
9) *Right-click any empty space on your desktop, click New, and then click Folder.*
10) *Open the folder and from the Edit menu, click Paste.*

*Your emails are now backed up. It's a good idea to do this on a regular basis.*

*You can also backup Outlook's data in much the same way. In this case, go to the File menu and click Data File Management. Then click Open Folder. From this point proceed as described in steps 7 to 10 above.*

The procedure in this page applies to only those of you using Microsoft Outlook as your email client.

Outlook saves its data (your emails) in a PST file, which is located at C:\Documents and Settings\Username\Application Data\ Microsoft\Outlook. Occasionally this file may become corrupted, with the result that emails are lost. Many people are unaware that Outlook has an inbox repair tool (Scanpst.exe) that can repair this PST file; although it must be said that it doesn't always work. It's worth a try though, and you can run it as described below:

1 Locate the Inbox Repair tool by going to C:\Program Files\ Common Files\System\MSMAPI\1033

2 Open the 1033 folder and click SCANPST.

![Inbox Repair Tool dialog box. Title: "Inbox Repair Tool". Text: "Enter the name of the file you want to scan:" with field showing "s\Username\Application Data\Microsoft\Outlook" and a Browse... button. Buttons at bottom: Start, Close, Options...]

3 Use the Browse button to locate Outlook's PST file at the address given at the top of this page. Then click Start.

The Inbox Repair tool will then scan the file and if it finds any damage will give you a prompt to repair the file. When this process is complete, open Outlook and look in the folder list for a "Lost and Found" folder. This folder will contain any data that the repair tool managed to recover.

# Where's the Volume Control?

Windows XP, by default, does not place the Volume Control in the Notification area of the Taskbar.

So, if you want it there – and it is handy – you'll have to do it yourself.

A known bug in Windows XP sometimes prevents the volume icon from appearing, even when the volume box is ticked. If this is the case try the following:

Log off Windows and then log back on again. See if it appears now. If it doesn't, right-click the Taskbar and select Task Manager. Under the Processes tab, highlight explorer.exe and click the End Task button. Then from the File menu click New Task, and in the box type explorer. Click OK.

1. Go to Start, Control Panel and click Sounds and Audio Devices.

**Sounds and Audio Devices Properties**

Tabs: Volume | Sounds | Audio | Voice | Hardware

VIA AC'97 Audio (WAVE)

Device volume

Low — High

☐ Mute

☑ Place volume icon in the taskbar

Advanced...

Speaker settings

Use the settings below to change individual speaker volume and other settings.

Speaker Volume... | Advanced...

OK | Cancel | Apply

The problem could also be that the volume icon is actually there, but is hidden from view by XP's "Hide inactive icons" feature.

Check this out by clicking the little arrow at the left of the taskbar tray. If you can see the volume control now then click the Start button and right-click the bottom of the Start Menu. Click Properties, click the Taskbar tab and then click Customize. In the Customize Notifications dialog box, double-click Volume and then, under Behavior, select Always Show. The volume icon will now always be visible.

2. Make sure the Volume tab is selected and then tick "Place volume icon in the taskbar."

Adobe Photoshop | Adobe InDesign CS 3... | 06:07

3. Single-click the volume control to increase, lower or mute the volume. Double-click for a wider range of options, such as Wave, Line-in and CD Player controls.

# XP Keeps Asking for the Install Disc

*Adding and removing Windows components with the Add and Remove Programs wizard in the Control Panel is an example of when a user will be asked for the Windows installation disc.*

While the above title maybe something of an exaggeration, it is a fact that most people will, at some time or other, be in the process of installing an application, only to see a message pop up asking them to put the Windows CD in the CD-ROM drive.

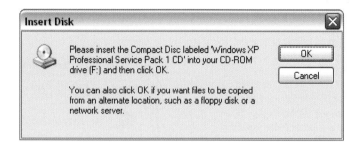

This happens because, for the application in question to work, certain files also have to be copied from the installation disc.

To prevent this happening, do the following:

*The i386 folder on the XP installation CD contains all the Windows files. This folder is some 446 MB in size.*

Place the XP installation disc in the CD-ROM drive. Then go to My Computer, right-click the CD-ROM drive icon and then click Open. This will reveal the contents of the disc.

2 Find the folder named i386, right-click it and click copy. Now go to your hard disk, right-click and select Paste. The i386 folder will now be copied to the drive.

*When it needs files from the installation disk, XP will by default go to the CD-ROM drive and look for the disc there.*

*By amending the registry, we are instructing it to look elsewhere – in this case the i386 folder on the hard drive.*

Now we need to edit the registry so that the system can find the files you have just transferred.

Open the registry by typing REGEDIT in the Run box in the Start menu.

2 Using the hierarchal tree on the left, locate the following entry: KEY_LOCAL_MACHINE\Software\Microsoft\WindowsNT\ CurrentVersion

3   Click the CurrentVersion folder.

When making changes in the registry, always make a backup copy before those changes are made. All you have to do is click the File menu and click Export.

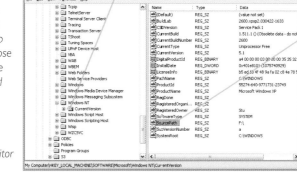

4   Double-click SourcePath.

5   In the Value Data box, alter the existing entry to read *C:\i386* (where C is your hard disk).

The registry editor has a useful search feature called Find, available from the Edit menu. This facility is very useful if you know what you are looking for.

6   Now find the following registry entry:
HKEY_LOCAL_MACHINE\Software\Microsoft\Windows\CurrentVersion\Setup

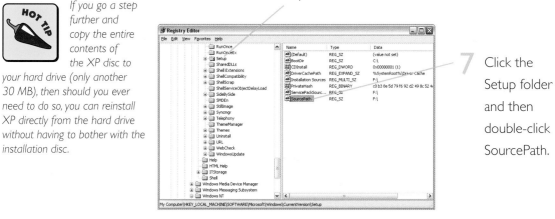

If you go a step further and copy the entire contents of the XP disc to your hard drive (only another 30 MB), then should you ever need to do so, you can reinstall XP directly from the hard drive without having to bother with the installation disc.

7   Click the Setup folder and then double-click SourcePath.

8   In the Edit string dialog box, change the existing setting to C:\

Close the registry editor and from now on you will never again be asked for the installation disc.

# XP Annoyances

*Microsoft's Error Reporting feature, is, in my opinion, a good thing. It gives Microsoft valuable information about what was happening on the system at the time of the crash, which can then be used to figure out what caused it. Future versions of Windows should then be less prone to crashes and errors.*

*For those of you concerned that information sent in this way may pose some sort of security risk, the following is taken from the Microsoft website:*

*"Error report data is used to find and fix problems in the software you use. It is not used for marketing purposes. When you submit an error report, we protect it through the use of encryption, such as the Secure Socket Layer (SSL) protocol. When we receive an error report, we use a variety of security technologies and procedures to help protect your personal information from unauthorized access, use, or disclosure. For example, we store the error reports you provide on computer servers with limited access.*

*Microsoft employees, contractors and vendors who have a business need to use the error report data are provided access. If the error report indicates that a third-party product is involved, Microsoft may send the data to the vendor of that product, who may in turn send the data to sub-vendors and partners."*

Although it is an excellent operating system, there are some aspects of XP that many users find irritating. This section details some of these and shows you how to disable them.

## Error Reports

Whenever an application crashes or locks-up and is closed down either by the user or by Windows, the XP Error reporting feature will pop up, asking if you want to report the error to Microsoft.

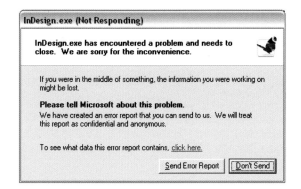

You can disable this as follows:

1 Go to Start, Control Panel and System. Click the Advanced tab. Under Startup and Recovery, click Error Reporting.

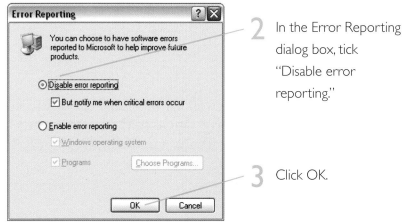

2 In the Error Reporting dialog box, tick "Disable error reporting."

3 Click OK.

When you install a new application in Windows XP, apart from the newly installed program message, the program's name is also highlighted in the All Programs menu, so that you can find it more quickly. This can be disabled as well.

1) Open the registry editor and locate the following entry: HKEY_CURRENT_USER\ Software\Microsoft\Windows\ CurrentVersion\Explorer

2) Create a new DWORD value named StartNotifyNewApps and set the value to 0 to disable the highlighting feature. To reenable it, change the value to 1.

## Newly Installed Program Messages

When these messages appear they obscure the All Programs, Log Off and Turn Off Computer buttons. As all they do is get in the way, and they serve no useful purpose, you can safely disable them.

1 Open the Start menu and right-click in the gray area at the top or bottom, then click Properties.

2 This opens the Taskbar & Start Menu Properties dialog box. On the Start menu tab, click Customize and then in the Customize Start Menu dialog box, click the Advanced tab.

3 Remove the check mark from the "Highlight newly installed programs" box.

While the information in many of XP's balloon tips is of little importance, occasionally it can be well worth knowing. A typical example is Delayed Write Failure error messages (see page 166) These alert a user to the fact that data is being corrupted. Disable balloon tips at your own risk.

## Balloon Tips

XP has an irritating habit of throwing up balloon tips, which give the user various types of information. Much of this is obvious or will already be known to the user.

For those of you who can manage without these tips, the solution is as follows:

*Another way of disabling balloon tips (and, indeed, many other of XP's irritations), is by installing and running TweakUI. This is one of Microsoft's Power toys, which can be downloaded from www.microsoft.com/windowsxp/pro/downloads/powertoys.asp*

*This utility enables users to make many adjustments to XP that would otherwise require tinkering with the registry or system files.*

1 Go to Start and click Search.

2 Scroll down the "What do you want to search for?" list until you see Change Preferences. Click this.

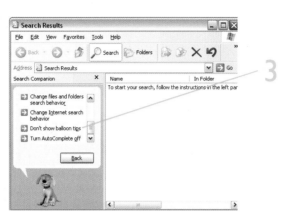

3 Scroll down until you see "Don't show balloon tips" and click it.

## XP's Unsigned Driver Warnings

XP doesn't like incompatible drivers and so warns you when you are installing a driver that has not been certified by Microsoft. If you don't want these messages though, they can be disabled.

*The purpose of XP's Driver Warning messages is to prevent the installation of software that can adversely affect general system stability. By heeding the warnings to not install the drivers you may be preventing problems such as:*

*1) Replacement of identically named files used by other devices or applications.*

*2) Version incompatibility that prevents other applications from running or that removes special capabilities of other devices.*

*3) System instability, when a poor-quality driver causes program errors or corrupts memory.*

1 Go to Start, Control Panel and System. Click the Hardware tab. In the Device Manager section, click Driver Signing.

2 Click "Ignore – install the software anyway and don't ask for my approval."

# XP Service Pack 2 Troubleshooting

The main purpose of Service Pack 2 (SP2) is to address the many security issues that have made XP so vulnerable to malicious attacks.

Microsoft have also included some other useful and well overdue features such as a browser pop-up blocker and a much improved automatic updates utility.

However, the overall emphasis on security issues has inevitably led to problems with certain types of application that are not yet compatible with SP2's more rigorous security demands.

This chapter explains the main features of SP2 and the problems users are likely to experience with it.

## Covers

**Chapter Fifteen**

# What's It All About?

The primary purpose of SP2 is to provide added security to XP. However, it also includes various enhancements to the operating system such as the latest versions of DirectX (version 9) and Windows Media Player.

Excellent operating system though it may be, major security deficiencies in the first release of Windows XP have proved to be a magnet to the perpetrators of viruses. Remember the MSBlaster worm that was doing the rounds not so long ago, which enabled the attacker to gain full access to a computer? Another flaw, in the Microsoft Java machine, has led to a plague of browser hijacking, while a loophole in XP's Messenger service has resulted in a flood of desktop spam.

Because the above issues (and others) have led to so many problems for users, SP2 is predominantly about plugging these security gaps. It's main features relate to:

XP's Messenger service, which has been responsible for unsolicited desktop spam (see page 163), is automatically disabled by SP2.

- Internet Explorer
- Outlook Express
- An updated firewall
- Automatic Updates
- Wireless networking support
- Bluetooth support

The main change to Internet Explorer is improved security that prevents websites from surreptitiously sending viruses, spyware, etc. to a user's machine.

Outlook Express is updated with an automatic HTML content blocking facility. This reduces the likelihood of receiving spam emails, by removing the loophole that alerts a spammer to the fact that your email address is an active one.

XP's Automatic Updates and Firewall utilities have been redesigned to persuade users to enable them. Doing so is a good move, as it helps to protect your system from the latest viruses.

SP2 updates XP's Internet Connection Firewall with an improved version, which is enabled by default and has many more options.

XP's Automatic Update utility is much improved, and as with the firewall, is now enabled by default. Also, new compression and patching technologies have reduced the size of patches, making it quicker to download and install them.

SP2 also provides a pop-up window blocker. This can be configured to block most or all pop-ups, but allow pop-ups from specified sites.

Setting up a wireless network is now much easier thanks to the new Setup Wizard. Wireless networking security is also much improved.

# SP2 & Internet Explorer

Loopholes within Internet Explorer have been the single biggest cause of security issues for users of Windows XP. One of the more well-known of these is a series of security controls that could be altered by a third party, thus rendering Internet Explorer and the computer open to a malicious attack. To resolve this issue and others, SP2 includes many patches designed to strengthen Internet Explorer's security capabilities.

 *Early indications are that many websites using applications such as ActiveX and Java do not function properly with SP2 even when the application in question is enabled by the user. There is little you can do about this – the problem can only be resolved by the webmaster, who will need to update the website to make it compatible with SP2's new security features.*

The downside of all these security enhancements, however, is that many web-based applications, such as ActiveX applets, downloads, pop-up windows and other script-based programs, may not work with SP2-enhanced Internet Explorer. By default, Internet Explorer is also now configured to disable many of these applications, although the user does have the option to manually reenable them.

When this type of problem occurs, Internet Explorer opens a yellow Information Bar, which details the problem and offers various options when clicked. This is demonstrated below:

*Another feature of SP2 is the Add-On Manager, available from the Tools menu in Internet Explorer. This allows you to manage the use of ActiveX controls and other browser applications.*

The Information Bar tells you that a pop-up window has been blocked and also that other content has been blocked to protect your security. Click the bar to get more details.

Usually the problem will be a site trying to download an ActiveX control, which has the potential to access data on a PC, install software or allow a computer to be remotely controlled. While in most cases the control will be quite innocuous, such as a Shockwave Flash object, it could be harmful.

By clicking the Information Bar, you will be given the option to install the software, but this should be done only if you are sure the site can be trusted. Prior to SP2, the software would have been automatically installed without your knowledge.

# SP2 & Outlook Express

*When Outlook Express detects external content, it will display a yellow Information Bar in the same way that Internet Explorer does. Clicking the bar gives you several options, including downloading the external content that was included with the message without having to enable the option in the Security Options.*

SP2 also includes security enhancements to Outlook Express. These make the handling of email safer by reducing the possibility of downloading a virus hidden in an email.

Another improvement to Outlook Express relates to the issue of spam email. Many people are unaware of the fact that many of these messages contain a link to a tiny single-pixel image on the spammer's web server. Previous versions of Outlook Express would automatically download this image when the email was opened, and because it is so tiny the user was unaware of it. When the request for the image was made to the web server, it confirmed to the spammer that the email was received by a valid email account. The result of this would be the reception of many more spam messages, from both the original spammer and new spammers to whom the email address was subsequently sold.

SP2 prevents this by adding a new option to Outlook Express's Security Options, as shown below.

*An added benefit of the external content blocking feature is that it minimizes a common problem experienced by dial-up users – undesired attempts to connect to the Internet.*

*Outlook Express would do this when an HTML email was viewed offline if it contained a reference to a web-based image. In an effort to retrieve the image, it would automatically dial out. However, because these images are now blocked by SP2, Outlook Express doesn't "see" them and so doesn't try and make a connection.*

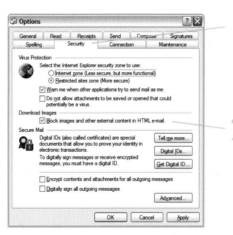

1   Go to the Tools menu in Outlook Express and select Options, Security.

2   The "Block images and other external content in HTML e-mail" option is enabled by default.

Remember, this new option is enabled by default and so all images and other content, legitimate or otherwise, contained in HTML emails will be blocked. In the case of images, this will result in an empty placeholder marked with a red X.

So, when you see this after installing SP2, don't assume it is a fault – it is done by design. However, if you are sure the content is safe to view you can disable the option (see Step 2 above).

# SP2 & Automatic Updates

Consistent with its "enhanced security" theme, SP2 urges users to select XP's Automatic Update feature on startup, and, if they don't, nags them with a pop-up message, as shown below.

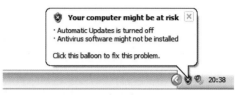

The reason for this is that, prior to SP2, Automatic Update was an option that the majority of users neglected to select, with the result that many computers were left vulnerable to attack.

Microsoft is hoping that the prompts will result in most users enabling the automatic option. If it works out as expected, this single measure alone should mean that many more computers are protected.

The user also has three other options with Automatic Update:

1) Download updates for me, but let me choose when to install them.

2) Notify me but don't automatically download or install them.

3) Turn off Automatic Updates.

However, due to a change in the way that Automatic Update works with SP2, option 1 above can cause the computer to take a long time to shut down. The reason for this is that Automatic Update is configured by default to install any downloaded updates before the PC is powered off. A message will appear at the bottom of the shutdown screen saying that "…. update" is being installed.

This is Microsoft attempting to make sure that updates are installed, in an effort to overcome user apathy. If the user really doesn't want to install the update, though, a "do not install" option is available at the bottom of the "Turn Off Computer" dialog box.

# Miscellaneous SP2 Issues

### Windows Firewall

SP2 delivers a new version of XP's Internet Connection Firewall, known simply as Windows Firewall. This comes with a user interface, unlike the ICF, which makes it easier to customize to your operating environment.

*Windows Firewall provides more safeguards than the ICF did. For example, the bootup and shutdown procedures are better protected. That said, it is still not as good as third-party firewalls such as Zone Alarm and Symantec's Personal Firewall. If either of these is available, disable Windows Firewall.*

You need to be aware that Windows Firewall is enabled by default, so if you are already using a third-party firewall, a decision needs to be made as to which one you want active – two active firewalls are likely to cause problems.

*If SP2 is installed on a system that wasn't previously running a firewall, the user may well suddenly experience connection problems when accessing the Internet. This is because SP2 will install and enable the Windows Firewall and its default settings are quite likely to be unsuitable for the user's operating environment.*

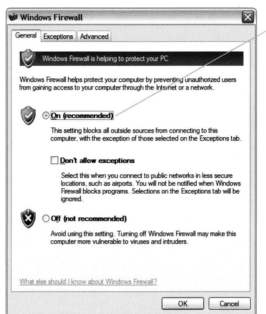

Windows Firewall is enabled by default.

*At the time of writing, Windows Security Center appears to be prone to errors. Until software manufacturers update their products to make them compatible with this utility, it might be as well to not place too much reliance upon it.*

### Windows Security Center

Windows Security Center is a new application, the purpose of which is to advise users when their system is not adequately protected with a firewall, anti-virus software and the latest Windows and Internet Explorer updates. The utility is accessible by clicking the red shield icon in the notification area.

Unfortunately, many users are reporting that Windows Security Center is not very reliable at detecting third-party security programs, which makes its usefulness somewhat questionable.

# Index